KNOWING YOUR DRESSM/

KNOWING YOUR DRESSMAKING

Maureen Goldsworthy, M.A.

Head of Needlework, Campion High School for Girls

Diagrams by Janet Watson

MILLS & BOON LIMITED, LONDON

First published 1973 by Mills & Boon Limited,
17–19 Foley Street, London W1A 1DR

Reprinted 1977 & 1979

© Maureen Goldsworthy 1973

ISBN 0 263 06418 2

Printed in Great Britain by Thomson Litho Ltd,
East Kilbride, Scotland
Bound by Hunter & Foulis, Edinburgh

CONTENTS

Note: In the diagrams throughout the book, shading has been used, where needed, to show the right side of the fabric, as in most well-known commercial patterns.

FOREWORD

Dear Reader,

Have you ever said, "Oh, I can make clothes, in a way—but they never fit, they take months to get finished, and then they look terrible?" If so, this book was written for you. It is about making clothes that really fit you, making fabrics behave as you want them to—and how to do it quickly.

Why *do* some home-made clothes "look terrible"? If you look carefully at good ready-made garments, you can see how they are put together, and how modern fabrics are managed. Think how you could use some of these ways in your own dressmaking. Many of the methods shown in this book are ones used in factories, to make top-quality clothes.

When you have learned dressmaking, a garment will not take months to finish. You will be able to go out in the morning, buy your pattern and fabric—and wear your dress that evening. Speed like this means not only *practice*, but also *knowing the right way*. This is the quickest and simplest way to get exactly the result you want. (That is, of course, *why* it is right.)

So if you have learned the basic sewing methods in KNOWING YOUR SEWING, you are now ready to learn some time-savers. One of the best of these is to *prepare properly* before machining. Time spent in pinning, tacking and fitting saves so much *more*, later. Never waste time, temper and good material by having to unpick!

Just one word of warning. If you are not sure what to do next, or how to do it, don't ask the very experienced dressmaker who lives just down the road. Either she may be so *very* experienced that her methods are too difficult for you—or, just possibly, she may not be nearly as good as you think she is. Either way, she may land you in a dreadful tangle. So look at your pattern instructions, ask your needlework teacher, (if you are at school or belong to an evening class), or work carefully from the book.

If you are working for an exam, this book can be used for O Level. In any case, I hope it will help you to look your best in well-made, up-to-the-minute, beautifully-fitting clothes.
Yours sincerely,

Maureen Goldsworthy

1 MAKE TO MEASURE

The secret of a good fit is **accurate measuring**. Clothes are uncomfortable and pull into creases if they are too tight—they look droopy and shapeless if too loose. With careful measuring and fitting, you can have a better garment than you could buy off the peg—because it has been made to your own measurements.

MEASURE YOURSELF

Bust   Measure a close fit, keeping the tape-measure high across your back, and over the widest part of the bust in front.

Waist   A snug fit, comfortable for a skirt waistband.

Hips   Measure round the widest part, 7"–9" (18–23 cm) below your waist. Do not allow any more for "ease"—a pattern in your size will give you 2" (5 cm) extra at bust and hip, for moving and sitting.

Back Waist Length   Measure from the bone you can feel at the back of your neck, down to your waist. Tie a string round your waist to find its exact level.

Sleeve Length   Bend your elbow; measure from shoulder to elbow, then on to wristbone.

Arm Width   With your elbow still bent, measure round your upper arm.

Crutch Depth   Sit down—now measure from your waist, over your hip, to the seat of the chair. This crutch measurement is needed for well-fitting trousers.

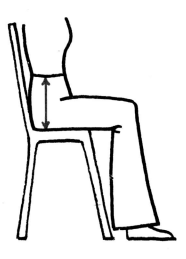

These are the basic measurements, and are nothing to do with changing fashion. They measure your bone structure, which does not change once you are full-grown. Even putting on or losing a pound or two in weight makes very little difference. Knowing these measurements, you can choose a pattern in your **bust size**, that also matches your **back waist length**, (and so suits your height). Get these two measurements right, and any other alterations you need will be simple ones.

MEASURE YOUR PATTERN

Too-loose patterns   Most patterns allow far too much room, so that the finished garment looks baggy. For beginners, the extra room may come in useful in case of accidents. But if you have already made a garment in, say, a size 12—and found that it hangs round you in folds—then make your next one in a size 10. It will be quite big enough, and give you a far better fit, even though it is meant for a smaller bust size.

To check the exact size of the pattern, measure across the half-pattern for the back, and the half-pattern for the front, at bust level (not counting in seam allowances).

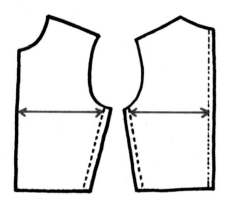

Double this to find the garment's bust measurement. It should be 2″ (5 cm) larger than your own. If it is 4″ (10 cm) larger, or more, you would do better with a smaller size.

Too-long patterns

Misses' patterns are long to the waist, to fit taller people of 5′ 5″ (165 cm) or more. They are also longer in the skirt and trouser leg. If you are less than about 5′ 7″ (170 cm) tall, you will probably need to shorten these patterns. Before buying your material, check the finished length of the garment, shown on the pattern envelope, and also look at the cutting layouts. If you are making a dress much shorter than the pattern allows for, you may be able to buy less fabric.

Young junior/Teen patterns are for shorter girls, about 5′ 2″ (157 cm), with figures still developing.

Junior petite patterns are for shorter girls, who are about 5′ 0″ (153 cm) tall, but full-grown and with developed figures. Most girls find that these last two sets of patterns need fewer alterations, and fit much better. Most makes of pattern have the same size ranges.

HOW TO ALTER YOUR PATTERN

1. The **back waist length** of the pattern must match yours, to be sure that the waistline comes in the right place. Alter, if you need to, on the pattern's lengthening and shortening line.

2. **Baggy armholes** are the worst and most common fault in home dressmaking. They pull up the whole side of your dress or jacket, when you raise your arm. A close-fitting armhole gives you a good line, no creases, and much more freedom of movement.

   The fault is usually in the pattern—and once your fabric is cut out, little can be done to put it right. So, to be on the safe side, always cut the armhole $\frac{3}{4}''$ (2 cm) **higher** under the arm, front and back, than the pattern allows. If this turns out to be too high, it can easily be trimmed off—but you cannot add it on once you have cut out.

3. Check the **sleeve width** around the upper arm. Some patterns are very tight here, and unless you are working with a stretchy fabric, you should allow 2″ (5 cm) more than your arm measurement, for ease in moving. Remember you may be wearing a sweater under a jacket—tight sleeves can be uncomfortable. Check also the **sleeve length**.

4. **Waist alterations** can be made by allowing a little extra at the sides of the pattern. $\frac{1}{2}''$ (1·2 cm) extra on each side edge, back and front, will make the finished waistline 2″ (5 cm) larger—a whole size.

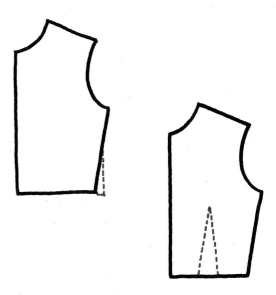

   For a smaller waist, make darts from the waistline upwards (and downwards on the skirt)—or enlarge the darts that are there already. Remember that **any** alteration above a waist seam will mean the same sized alteration below it.

5. **Hip alterations** are made by adding not more than $\frac{1}{2}''$ (1·2 cm) all down each side-seam.

Or by cutting the pattern and spreading it apart. (Do not cut through waist dart markings.)

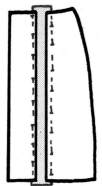

For smaller hips, pleat the pattern, avoiding darts.

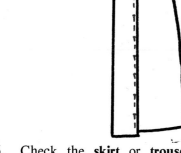

6. Check the **skirt** or **trouser length** from waist to hem—if in doubt, leave an extra inch. Trousers **must** be as long as possible for a good line.

7. **Crutch depth.** Alter the pattern at hip level, so that the crutch depth is the same as yours. If in doubt, cut the crutch level high —you can always trim it down later.

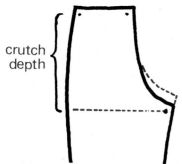

crutch depth

8. **Trouser leg width.** Any shaping below the knee depends on fashion. A flared trouser leg can easily be made from a straight-leg pattern. Simply add $\frac{3}{4}''$ (2 cm) extra width at the bottom of each leg and taper it away to nothing at knee level, about 17″ (43 cm) up from the hem.

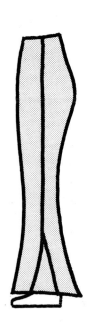

If a really wide flare is wanted, it is better to use a straight-leg pattern, but to put in the extra width as a godet (see page 65) in the side seam.

MEASURE THE STRAIGHT GRAIN

The warp threads of your fabric, parallel to the selvedge, are on the **straight grain**. In jersey fabrics, the grain goes along the wale, or rib, of the knit. All main pattern pieces should be placed on the fabric with the arrow running along the straight grain. Make sure of this as you pin down the pattern—the garment will not hang level if the grain is off-true. You might even get this lop-sided look.

So measure from one end of the arrow to the selvedge; then from the other end to the selvedge—both measurements should be exactly the same.

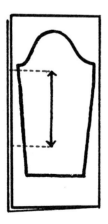

Smaller pieces, such as collars and pockets, are sometimes placed with their grain arrows at

right angles to the selvedge, instead of parallel to it.

Cutting "on grain" is so important for a good result, that you MUST NOT HURRY in pinning out the pieces. Extra time spent on checking is never wasted.

A **bent arrow**, pointing to the pattern's edge, means you must place that edge on—right on—a lengthwise fold of your fabric. If you place it $\frac{1}{2}''$ (1·2 cm) short of the fold, you will get a garment piece $1''$ (2·5 cm) bigger than you were expecting. (This is one way of making a pattern larger—but beware. Folds usually come down the middle of a garment; so if you enlarge it there, you may get a wide, sagging neckline as well.)

HOW TO KEEP THESE MEASUREMENTS RIGHT

Cut accurately on the thickly-printed cutting line. If you have made any alterations, draw them on the pattern and cut them exactly.

Notches (or balance marks) are the matching-points along seams, to show how each piece fits to the next one. They are to save you trouble in fitting; but if they are cut even slightly out of place, they can make puckers down a seam. You need not cut down between double notches, but you must make the *outside* corners sharp and clean, so that you can match them *exactly.*

Mark accurately the positions of darts, button-holes, etc. You will need to check these when you try on the garment.

Use tailor's tacks, really the safest and quickest way to mark a double thickness of fabric. Don't put in more than you need—but those you *do* use must be accurately placed. Take two stitches at the same spot, using a double thread, and leaving a loop big enough to put your finger through. Cut the thread between two or more tacks and lift off the pattern, tearing it as little as possible.

Pull the two thicknesses of fabric gently apart, and snip the threads between them. This will leave double tufts of thread in each piece, marking them both in exactly the same place.

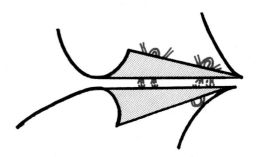

Instead of tailor's tacks, you can use a tailor's chalk pencil on top of the fabric and a chalk block underneath, to mark the double thickness. Another way is to use a sharp-edged tracing wheel and two layers of dressmaker's carbon paper (one underneath the folded fabric) to leave a coloured line on each thickness. There are two problems with both these ways of marking—they do not show well on thick, woolly fabrics, and the marks may not wash out of thin, pale-coloured ones. So be sure you mark on the wrong sides only.

Stay-stitch the edges of necklines and armholes, to stop them stretching out of shape while you are trying on and making up the garment. Once a V-neckline or an armhole has sagged it is very difficult to get back its proper shape. Stay-stiching is a line of straight machining $\frac{1}{2}''$ (1·2 cm) from any edge cut on the cross or bias, and just through a single thickness. It must be done **as soon as you have finished cutting out and marking.** It will not show because it will come inside the seam turnings.

Fabrics that fray badly can lose half their seam allowances before you even stitch the seams, if you are not careful. It is safest to stay-stitch straight after cutting out, then neaten all round, at the very edge, with zig-zag machining. Use a long stitch (a short one can stretch your fabric) and as wide as you can without making the edges curl up. Or overcast.

The five kinds of basting to make sure of a perfect fit.

(a) **Tacking**   This is done exactly on the fitting (or stitching) line, to hold two layers of fabric together until they are machine-stitched. Most seam allowances are $\frac{5}{8}''$ (1·5 cm). Most tape measures are also $\frac{5}{8}''$ wide; so an easy way to be exact is to lay one edge of your tape along the edge of the material, then pin level with the other edge of the tape.

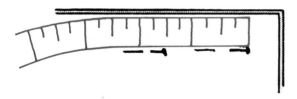

Now **tack** along the line of pins.

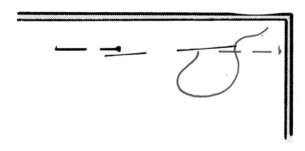

Begin with a firm, large knot or two back-stitches—and end with two back-stitches. Tacking that comes apart at each end, when you try on the garment, is useless. It also wastes your precious time when it has to be re-done.

(b) **Machine basting** (stitching with the very longest stitch your machine will do) is better on straight seams than tacking by hand—**if you can be perfectly accurate**. Use a different colour, and loosen the top thread a little, to make unpicking easier. Stitch just a thread away from the fitting line—the basting will not then get caught into the final machine stitching. Machine basting is also useful for holding together the opening edges of a garment, while you are setting in a zip.

(c) **Basting**, with stitches at right angles to the seamline, is to keep the two layers of fabric exactly **level**, so that they cannot slip during machining—as when you are matching checks or setting in a zip.

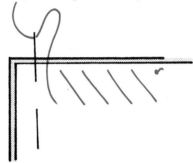

(d) **Pin-basting** is just the same as basting, but with pins instead of thread. Use it on the **wrong** side to match checks, or before machine-basting.

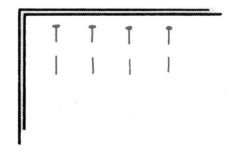

You can machine straight over the pins
if you go slowly,

if the pins are exactly at right angles to the stitching—and

if the fabric is thick enough to cushion the pins as they go through the machine. This is the only way you should ever machine-stitch over pins.

Pin-basting can also be used on the **right** side to hold a seam you have altered in fitting, until you stitch it.

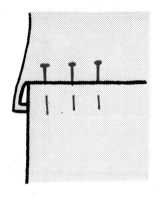

(e) **Slip-basting** is done on the right side of the garment, if you need to alter it during fitting. It is a great time-saver. Pin-baste the seam in place; then slip-baste, taking stitches first through one layer of the garment, then through the **fold** of the other layer.

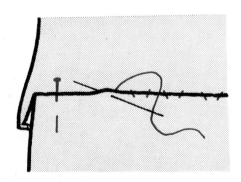

Then turn to the wrong side, and you are ready to machine with no further tacking. This is especially useful for curved seams.

Always use cotton threads for tacking and basting—polyester threads are too strong for the job, and will not easily break when you are ready to take them out.

Taping seams   Any seam that is cut on the cross-grain may stretch. Stay-stitching may not be enough to hold the shape of heavy fabrics or stretchy knits. So when you machine the two garment pieces together, stitch into the seam a piece of seam-binding or narrow ribbon. This will make a completely firm shoulder seam.

If you want just a **little** stretch, for an armhole seam, use bias binding instead; but stitch it just **within** the seam allowance, press it towards the armhole, and then stitch the sleeve into the armhole afterwards. You can save time, too, by using this binding to neaten the armhole.

The seams of **Raglan** sleeves always need taping, as they are cut on the cross from neckline to underarm.

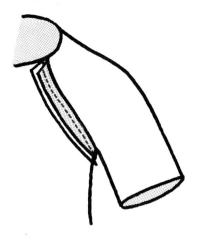

The underarm seam of a **Dolman** or Bat-wing sleeve will need taping for strength.

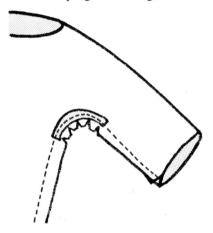

Machining in the right place   Here are some tips to keep you straight.

(a) **The presser-foot** of your machine will have the inside edges of its toes cut into different widths.

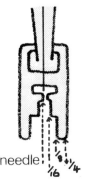

From the needle to the **outside edge** of the toe is probably $\frac{1}{4}''$ (6 mm)—to the **inside edges** may be $\frac{1}{16}''$ and $\frac{1}{8}''$ (2 and 3 mm). Use the toe to keep the edge of your fabric straight when you are edge-stitching, or sewing in a zip. Moving the needle to the left-hand position (on a swing-needle machine) will give you another, wider measurement. Put your tape-measure under the machine foot, to check the distances on **your** machine.

(b) **The needle-plate** on your machine probably has guide-lines marked on the right-hand side, at different distances from the needle.

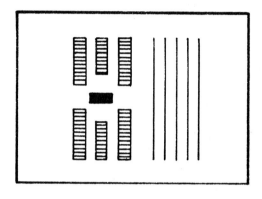

Measure the distance of each line from the needle. It is simple to keep the edge of your fabric level with your chosen line—and you will have a perfectly-placed seam. Watch the edge of the fabric, not the needle, as you stitch.

(c) If your needle-plate has no guide-lines, it may help you to stick on a strip of Sellotape or stamp-paper, with its left-hand edge $\frac{5}{8}''$ (1·5 cm) away from the needle. Then you can keep your fabric level with this.

(d) On most machines, you can screw an edge-guide into the needle-bar, and set it as far from the needle as you want. This is useful for wider measurements, but can be clumsy and get in your way for seams.

17

2 FIT TO BUST

If you have measured and cut accurately you should have little difficulty with fitting. Many garments, of course, do not have to fit closely all over. But **all** garments must fit well **somewhere**—usually at neck and bust—or they will look shapeless and ugly.

The secret is to work, step by step, from the top downwards. You may be able to leave out many of these steps in fitting—no one garment could possibly need all the alterations shown. But these are the ones most often needed, and easiest to make.

PREPARING FOR THE FIRST FITTING

1. Tack down the **centre front** and **centre back** lines of the garment (unless there is a centre seam). This "trace tacking" goes exactly down the straight grain, and will show if the garment hangs level on you.

2. Stitch any **seams** that you are sure will not need altering. A straight centre back or front seam may be stitched now, and a centre zip put in.

3. Tack all **darts**.

4. Tack up the **seams** of the whole garment, except for the sleeves, collar and facings. Include all **interfacings** (page 31) except those in hems. (Interfacings can be basted either to the garment or to the facings. Make sure you support, either by interfacing or by stay-stitching, any edge that might pull or stretch.)

5. Tack a firm Petersham ribbon to **skirt** or **trouser waist**, to support it properly. This can become part of the finished waistline, or it can be replaced by a waistband.

6. Tack **sleeve** and **collar** seams, but do not stitch them, or tack them to the garment, yet.

THE FIRST FITTING

For all garments—to check size and seams.

If you have measured yourself, and altered the pattern carefully before cutting out, only small alterations will be needed in fitting. You should be able to make these in seams and darts.

1. It is just possible for you to fit yourself, without anyone to help you—but it is difficult to stand relaxed, and yet be able to see what alterations are needed, front and back. It is also a very slow job, as you will have to take off the garment for each pinning. Get a friend to help you, if at all possible.

2. Wear the bra, and height of heel, that you expect to go with the garment.

3. Try it on, right side out. Zip up or pin together any openings.

4. Take a long look at yourself to get the general effect. Move about, and sit, to get used to the feel of the garment. Do not hurry to make alterations until you are sure what needs to be done.

5. To check the "balance", make sure that the **trace tacking** runs straight downwards, not towards the left or right side. If necessary, lift and pin one shoulder seam (or one side of the waistline), the *least* amount that will bring the trace tacking to hang straight down the centre.

6. Check that the **side seams** run straight towards the ground and do not curve forwards (or backwards). Correct by lifting the back (or front), at the shoulders or waistline, the **least** amount that will let the seams hang straight. If this balance is put right now, it will save making many more alterations later.

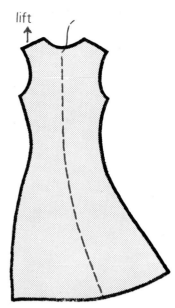

lift

7. Always make the **smallest alteration** that will let the garment hang easily and without pulling. Make two small alterations, for instance in two darts, rather than one large one. Use common sense in deciding how much to alter—do not over-fit, as you must have plenty of room to move.

8. **To alter**, snip the tacking thread of the seam, and pin-baste it into its new position.

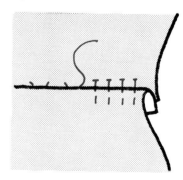

9. Slip-baste on the outside along the new seam-line (see page 16), before taking out the pins. This holds the new line firmly until you machine. Now try on the garment again, to be certain.

DANGER SIGNALS

"Fitting" is more than just making a garment the right size for you. It also means getting rid of any ugly creases that spoil the "set" or smooth lines of a flattering outfit. Watch for these danger signals:

Tight creases across the body   The garment, or part of it, is too tight. Let it out at the nearest side seams.

Loose folds hanging downwards **mean that the** garment is too wide—take it in at the nearest dart or side seam.

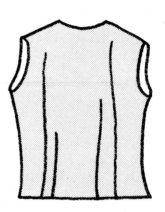

Tight creases pulling up-and-down   Part of the garment is too short. Let it out at the nearest seam **above** the creases.

Loose folds drooping across the garment show that part of it is cut too long—take it up in the nearest seam **above** the folds.

FITTING A DRESS, JACKET OR BLOUSE

1. **Width of the neckline** The back of the neckline should fit snugly. If it is **too loose,** make darts at the back neck, about 4″ (10 cm) long—longer if they look right. Or take in a centre back seam.

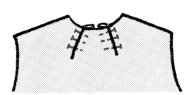

   For a **too-tight** neckline, clip inwards from the edge $\frac{1}{4}″$–$\frac{1}{2}″$ (about 1 cm) until it settles down comfortably. Or let out the shoulder seams.

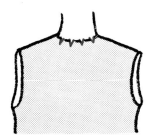

   Remember that either of these alterations will mean shortening or lengthening any facings or collar.

2. **Height of the neckline** One that is too high at the back will make wrinkles or folds form across the centre back, just below the neck. Clip the tacking of the shoulder seams on each side of the neck, trim the back neck edge a little lower, and re-pin the seams to lift out the wrinkles.

clip tacking, trim and lift

3. **To smooth out the shoulder line**, alter the outer ends of the shoulder seams. If you are using shoulder pads, they should be pinned in first.

   Make sure the seam lies along the top of the shoulder. For **square shoulders,** let out the ends of the seams—for **sloping shoulders**, take them in.

lift

4. When you are quite happy with the fit of the neck and shoulders, draw a tailor's chalk line around the neck, to mark where the **neckline seam** is to be. This should pass over the bone at the back of the neck.

5. **Darts below the bust** Make sure that any darts run directly up towards the point of the bust, and finish about $1\frac{1}{2}″$ (4 cm) below it. Darts must look the right size—wide enough to make a good shape, but not so wide that the bodice puffs out above them.

6. **Underarm darts** These should also point towards the bust—quite a small alteration in the angle of the dart will make all the difference to the fit of a bodice. This is a very important part of fitting, because the

position of darts shows up clearly on the finished garment.

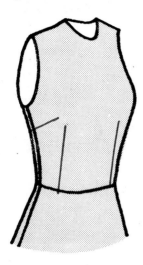

7. **Height and level of waistline** Tie a string around your waist to mark where a belt would be. If there is a waist seam, make sure it is level and at the right height. Mark the placing for any belt-carriers (see page 93).

8. **Width around the body** Make any alterations at the side seams. There should be enough room for the garment not to wrinkle up when you move—but not so much that it hangs around you like a sack. It should make a good smooth line on you.

9. **Now check the armholes** The top of the armhole seam should come at the point of the shoulder. (This is the bone you will feel if you run your fingers up the outside of your arm.) Chalk a fitting line for the seam round the armhole; from the point of the shoulder—straight down the front edge— as high as comfortable under the arm— and up the back to the shoulder again. This is the line to which you will fit your sleeve.

10. **Try on a sleeve**, but do not pin it in yet. Check the width round the upper arm, and the length. A tailored sleeve in a jacket is safer left with the wrist end unfinished until you have set it into the armhole. Other sleeves, especially those gathered into cuffs, are easier to manage if the wrist ends are finished **before** setting them in.

11. If there is a **front opening**, check that it does not gape or pull at the cross-over. You may have to alter slightly at the front edge of the shoulder seams, or at the back of the neck (altering also the collar), to make a good line over the bust. Be careful —it is easy to over-fit here. If in doubt, leave it.

12. **Front buttoning** Chalk in the placing and levels of the buttonholes. One should be on the waistline (unless there is a belt) and one at the widest part of the bust.

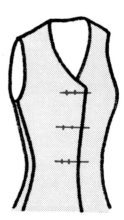

13. The placing and size of **pockets** should be decided now. Pin paper shapes of different pockets to the garment, until you are pleased with the effect. Mark their positions on one side of the garment. Fold it in half and make tailor's tacks through both halves, to match the pockets exactly.

14. **A back vent in a jacket** should hang

straight and closed. If the two sides gape open,

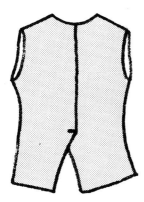

nip in the **centre back** seam at and just above the waist. Let out the **side seams** below the waist and over the hips.

1. Fit the **waist** by altering the size or number of darts, and ending them just above the hip-line.
2. The width round the **hips** should give enough room to move and sit comfortably. Let out or take in the side seams.
3. If there are **pleats**, make sure they hang straight. Gaping pleats may need to be supported (page 64) or lifted at waist level.

If this does not work, let out the side seams from the hips downwards.
4. Check that the hem edge is hanging level. If not, lift the back or front of the skirt at the waistline, re-pinning it to the waist petersham.

5. Decide now the placing of any **pockets** that are to be set into seams. They are best set high, so that their tops are sewn into the waist finish, (page 74).

FITTING TROUSERS

The best way to make successful trousers is to choose the right fabric. Make sure there is *some* give or stretch in it, or the trousers will be more difficult to fit and less comfortable to wear. Check also that the material is really smooth—a scratchy tweed might make you itch, and could become quite unwearable.

Double jerseys and warp-knits (see page 49) are good for trousers because they stretch sideways, but not so much downwards—so they will give you a good fit, but will not bag at the seat and knees.

1. The **Petersham ribbon** at the waist must be firmly tacked on.

2. Try sitting down. Make sure that the **crutch** is high enough to be comfortable on you, sitting or standing. A crutch set too low pulls across the front, is uncomfortable to wear, and makes your legs look shorter. Lift the whole garment on the waist petersham.

   But if the crutch looks like this it is **too** high, and needs to be dropped (see page 12).

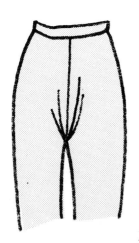

3. Check that the **side seams** run straight downwards. If they slant forwards on the leg, lift the back waistline a little (or drop the front) and re-pin to the petersham.

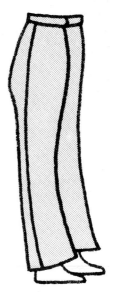

If they hang towards the back, lift the front a little.

4. Check that the **trouser legs** hang evenly each side of your legs.

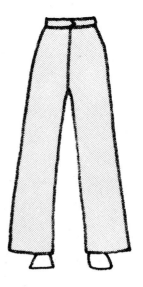

Lift or drop at the **sides** of the waistband until they do.

5. Trousers may droop at the **back of the waist**, making a hollow in the small of the back. It will help to lift the garment on the waistband at the centre back.

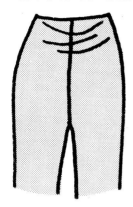

6. To **fit the waist** snugly, alter the darts, as for a skirt.

7. Make sure the width round the **hips** is right. 1″ (2·5 cm) is enough for ease, if the trousers are comfortable to sit in and there are no tight creases. If too loose, take in the side seams. If too tight, let them out all the way down, to keep a smooth hip line—or let out the centre back seam.

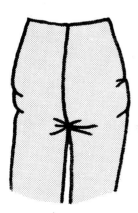

8. Check the width round the **thighs**. 1″ (2·5 cm) of ease is enough, if comfortable, and

will avoid ugly pulled creases. Trousers can be drum-tight only if they are made of a stretch fabric. Let out or take in equally on the outside and inside leg seams.

25

AFTER THE FIRST FITTING

1. Stitch all the **darts and seams** you have just checked. Include any belt-carriers or pockets in seams. Press.

2. Neaten all the seams, unless the garment is to be lined.

3. Set in any **zip** or fastening not already sewn in.

4. Put in the **lining** of a skirt (page 35), and set on the **waistband** of a skirt or trousers.

5. Make up the **collar**. (If you altered the neckline, you may need to alter the collar size.) Tack it in place at the neckline.

6. Attach the **facings**.

7. Make **bound buttonholes**.

8. Make and attach **pockets** (see page 71).

9. Run two rows of machine gathering round each **sleeve-head**, one just inside and one just outside the fitting line.

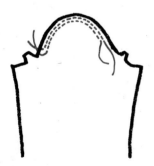

   Make up the **sleeves** and finish the wrist ends. Pull up the gathering threads until the sleeve fits the armhole. Press and shape the sleeve-head with the tip of the iron, to smooth out any wrinkles (page 59).

10. On the wrong side, pin and tack the sleeve into the armhole, matching the underarm seams, and tacking only as far as the front and back notches. Do *not* join on the sleeve above the notches, yet.

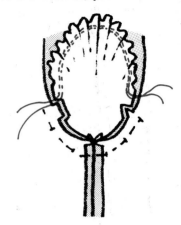

11. Press the whole garment lightly on the wrong side.

THE SECOND FITTING

1. Check the set of the **collar**. Does it fit the neckline? Does it roll over in a smooth line?

2. Check that **zips** or other fastenings lie flat.

3. On a skirt or trousers, see that the **waistline** is smooth. Mark the positions for waistband hooks and eyes.

4. Decide the **skirt length** and pin up the hem. This is much easier if the hem edge was levelled at the first fitting.

5. For **trousers**, the longer they can be, the more flattering the line. Shape them up over the foot in front, and down behind, for a longer leg line. At the side seams, they should come down at least to the ankle bone.

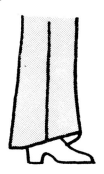

FITTING SLEEVES

1. Spread the sleeve-head gathers evenly across the head of the sleeve.

2. Now fold in the sleeve seam allowance between the rows of gathers, down as far as the notches, so that the sleeve fitting-line comes on the fold.

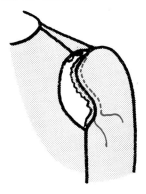

Pin-baste this fold to the outside of the armhole, catching in just a few threads of the fold, and pinning to the armhole fitting line. Match the centre mark of the sleeve-head to the shoulder seam, and pin down the front and back of the armhole as far as the notches.

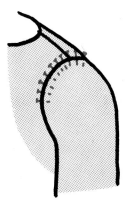

As the pins are all on the outside of the shoulder, they can easily be moved during the fitting, even if you are fitting yourself without any help.

3. See if the sleeve drags at the armhole. Tight creases like these mean that a little more of the sleeve seam-turning should be let out. Re-pin until the creases go.

4. Loose folds like these mean that the sleeve-top is too long—turn more of it into the seam.

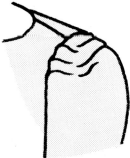

5. Creases pulling across the front of the sleeve, and loose folds at the back, mean that the gathers need to be moved a little towards the **front**, to swing the whole sleeve-top round slightly. The creases will go when it has been moved enough.

6. Creases pulling the other way (from the front, sloping towards the back), mean that the gathers should be moved **back** a little.

7. Sleeves with very full tops may need to be darted or pleated before pinning into the armhole. Make sure that the pleats are evenly spaced behind and in front of the shoulder seam, and that both sleeves match.

8. When you are satisfied with the fit of the sleeve, slip-baste it in place and remove the pins.

9. **Raglan** sleeves have a dart along the top of the shoulder, and **Dolman** sleeves have a seam there. They are fitted by taking in, or letting out, the dart or seam.

AFTER THE SECOND FITTING

1. Stitch and finish the collar and neck facings. (Page 66.)

2. Make machine or hand-worked button-holes. Sew on buttons.

3. Stitch in the sleeves.

4. Finish the inside of trousers, where the seams cross at the crutch, with a 3″ (8 cm) square of lining fabric, stitched only to the seam turnings. This gives a neat finish and better wear.

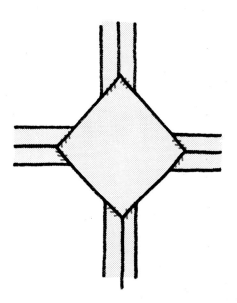

5. Finish the hems, and the lower ends of facings. Facings always fold **over** hems. On **thick** fabrics, trim down the part of the hem hidden by the facing, to get rid of bulk. Slip-stitch the edges together—(this

is like slip-basting, page 16, but smaller) —then herring-bone the facing over the hem.

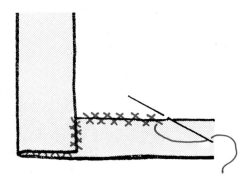

On **thin** fabrics, fold the facing to the **right** side, machine along the level of the hem.

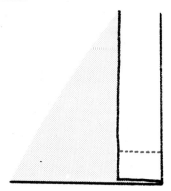

Turn the facing in, to the wrong side, and **slip-hem**, picking up only a thread or two from the garment, and then **slipping** the needle along inside the fold of the hem.

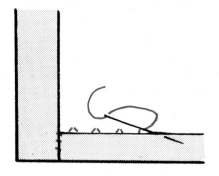

6. Give the garment a final, careful pressing —but do not over-press. Avoid flattening hem edges into sharp creases. Take care not to press over the top edge of a hem, or it might show as a ridge on the right side —and do not risk making any shiny marks with a too-hot iron.

7. Put in the lining of a jacket or coat (see page 39).

3 INTERFACING

Interfacing is used to support or give "body" to part of a garment. It stiffens the collar and revers of a tailored jacket, or strengthens the button placings on a shirt. Properly interfaced, a garment will always keep its line and stay the shape you made it.

INTERFACING MATERIALS

Choose the one that will suit your fabric.

Tailor's canvas is used for heavy wool fabrics, to be made into coats or tailored jackets. It gives body and support without stiffness. Do not use it in garments that will be washed. It can be bought in lighter or heavier qualities, to suit the weight of the garment fabric.

Vilene   This is not a woven fabric, but bonded —so it has no grain or stretch. Use it for washable garments.

There are many different thicknesses of Vilene, to suit any woven material except the very finest. It gives more stiffness than you would think from feeling it, so the lighter weights are the most useful;

A34—An extra light-weight, for *sheers* such as voile.
A40—A light-weight for *dress cottons*.
A50—A medium weight for *woollens* or *corduroy*.

244—A light-weight Terylene Vilene, for use with man-made materials.

There are also **iron-on Vilenes**, to use on small parts of a garment. Do not use them on the larger pieces, as the edge of the stiffened part would show clearly;

F2—A light-weight, which can be ironed onto **neckline** and **front facings**.
F3—A heavier weight, for small parts such as **pocket welts**, which must be really stiff.

The heat of the iron melts the "fusible" backing, and makes it stick to the fabric—when your iron is hot enough. Go on pressing until the Vilene goes "see-through" (like cooking bacon-fat); then it is hot enough to stick. Be very careful not to iron odd bits of Vilene onto your ironing board cover—or worse still, the wrong way up onto the sole-plate of your iron. (If you do, you can scrape it off, when cold, with a smooth knife-blade.)

Staflex   These are the interfacings most widely used in the dress trade. Made from woven, iron-on cotton fabric, they have some "give" on the bias, and make much the best stiffening for collars and revers. Also very useful ironed onto facings—in fact, this is how most ready-made garments are now interfaced. The even more useful **Knitted Staflex**—a thin, iron-on cotton jersey—is the best interfacing of all for knits, as it stretches with the fabric. It can also be used on woven materials. Unfortunately,

Staflex is not sold in shops, but it is worth the trouble of getting it by post from:

MacCulloch & Wallis, Ltd.,
25–26 Dering Street,
London W1R 0BH.

Organdie   A crisp, sheer cotton, used for interfacing cotton fabrics. As it creases, use it only on fabrics that have to be ironed in any case—NEVER on drip-dry ones.

Nylon Tricot—the fabric used for slips—makes a good interfacing for light-weight jersey fabrics, as it is stretchable and will not spoil the soft lines of knitted garments. Most thin knits are of man-made fibres, so nylon tricot will suit their washing instructions.

Non-iron sheer fabrics, such as terylene lawn: the best interfacing is an extra thickness of the fabric itself—for instance, in a blouse collar.

HOW TO USE INTERFACING

Front edges of a shirt or blouse   Put a narrow strip of Vilene or organdie inside the facing. If there is a seam, the interfacing is stitched into it —otherwise, the buttons or buttonholes hold it in place.

Collars and cuffs of thin fabric   Make them up in three thicknesses; two of the garment material, right sides together—and the third of interfacing, laid on top, and with its corners trimmed off. (This makes it easier to get sharply pointed corners when you turn it right side out.)

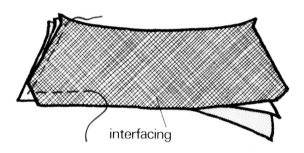

interfacing

Seam these three thicknesses together; trim the interfacing right down to the seam, and the outer fabric slightly wider, in layers.

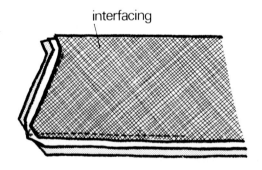

interfacing

Turn right side out and press. The interfacing will be held between the two layers of fabric.

To get a perfect finish round the edges of a collar, interfaced or not, first roll the seam over between your finger and thumb, then tack and press so that it lies just **under** the edge of the collar and will not be seen in wear.

Waistbands and pocket welts As these need to be stiff, use a heavy or Iron-on Vilene. Cut it to **half** the width of the waistband or welt, and slip-herringbone it along the fold. Trim off any Vilene inside the seam turnings, to get rid of bulk.

Tailored collars, revers and front facings of thicker jackets and coats. Use a fairly heavy interfacing—Vilene, Staflex or canvas—to hold the shape of the garment. Collar interfacing should be cut on the **bias** to roll over well; so do not use Vilene there.

Tack the interfacing to the under-collar and garment pieces; then hold it in place with Padding Stitch:

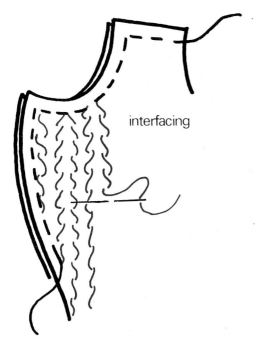

interfacing

Take very small stitches, through the inter-facing but not **right** through the thickness of the

outer fabric. The stitches should be in rows, from top to bottom and then back again, with about $\frac{1}{4}''$ (6 mm) between rows.

Hold the material curved over your hand as you sew, to help set the rolled-over line of collar and revers. This takes time, but gives such a good result that it is worth the trouble.

Or use Staflex or Knitted Staflex, ironed on over a tailor's pad or firmly rolled towel.

Staflex and Vilene can be stitched into the facing, neckline and shoulder seams of a garment, and trimmed off close to the seam. But canvas is too thick to treat like this; so trim off its seam-turnings and catch its edges in place with tiny herring-bone stitches, just $\frac{1}{8}''$ (3 mm) short of the seamlines.

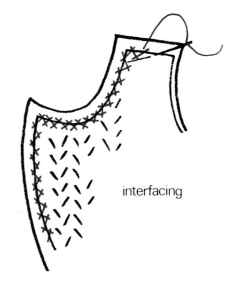

interfacing

For making up tailored collars and revers, see page 69.

Jacket and sleeve hems   Lay a strip of interfacing inside the hemline before turning it up. Cut the interfacing strips on the bias, to give a little stretch to the garment edge. To join the strips, simply overlap them, flat, and tack them together. The top edge should be slip-herring-boned loosely to the garment.

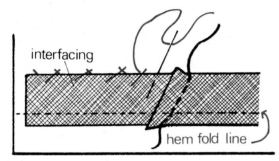

The lower edge will turn up in the fold of the hem. Stitch the hem to the interfacing only, not right through to the garment. When finished, the lining will hide the interfacing.

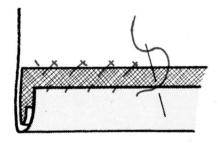

Sometimes a sleeve, in checked fabric, will be cut on the bias; then, it is better to cut the cuff interfacing on the **straight grain**—or use Vilene—so that the wrist edge does not stretch too much.

4 LINING

A lining helps clothes to shed creases, to hang well on the figure, and to slip on easily without pulling at the sleeves and shoulders. It can also keep you warm, or stop a dress from showing through.

You need not **neaten** the seam-turnings inside a fully-lined garment, as there will be no wear or rubbing on them. Just clip in the seam edges $\frac{1}{4}''$ (6 mm) every few inches, to stop long threads from ravelling off. Or use pinking shears—one of the few places where you should. Only neaten if the fabric is in a very open, fraying weave, or if the seam-turnings are narrow.

LINING FABRICS

These should be thinner than the garment they line. Use a firm fabric, such as Tricel taffeta, to keep the shape of the garment—especially to stop a skirt from "seating".

Some **knitted** fabrics are better without linings, just worn over a well-fitting slip; but if a lining is needed, try a slippery knit, such as a nylon tricot. It should have just enough stretch to keep the soft look that belongs to jersey fabrics.

Check that linings can be **washed** in the same way as their garments. Any lining that needs to be ironed should not be put into a drip-dry garment.

LINING A SKIRT

1. Cut the lining to the same pattern as the skirt, but about 2″ (5 cm) shorter. Stitch the darts and seams of the skirt, and set in the zip. Make up the lining separately. Now put the lining inside the skirt (wrong sides facing), and join them together in the waistband.

2. Turn in and **slip-stitch** the opening edges of the lining over the zipper tapes.

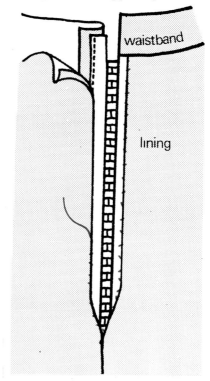

35

3. Turn up the hem of the lining **away** from the body, towards the skirt.

4. If there are pleats in the skirt, cut the lining short enough to keep the freedom of movement that pleats give you.

5. A half-lining, across the skirt back only, is better than nothing; it will help to stop the skirt from seating. Stitch the lining into the side seams of the skirt, with its wrong side towards the skirt back. Join the top into the waist seam.

LOOSE-LINING A DRESS

1. Make up the dress and lining separately, to the same pattern.

2. Stitch the lining to the neck of the dress, right sides together, as you would put on a neck facing. Turn it to the inside. Now fold under the raw edges down each side of the opening, and slip-stitch them to the dress turnings or zipper tape. Round the armholes, tack the lining to the bodice, and stitch it into the armhole seam when you set in the sleeve.

3. Dress sleeves are not usually lined.

4. If there is a waist seam, fold back the skirt and **tack** together the waist seam turnings of the lining and dress.

5. Turn up the hem of the lining separately, making it about 2″ (5 cm) shorter than the dress.

LINING A SLEEVELESS BODICE

This is a quick way to line a bodice and finish the neck and armhole edges, all by machine. It is also useful for baby clothes. Use it only where there is a neckline opening at a centre seam.

1. For the lining, use a neck and armhole facing cut as one piece.

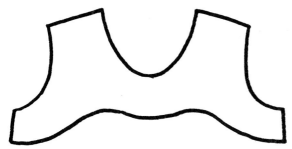

2. Stitch the shoulder seams **only** of the bodice.

3. Stitch the shoulder seams **only** of the facing.

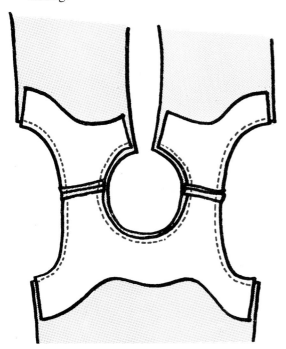

4. Match the bodice and facing, with right sides together.

5. Tack and stitch round the armholes and neckline.

6. Clip and layer the seam edges along the curves.

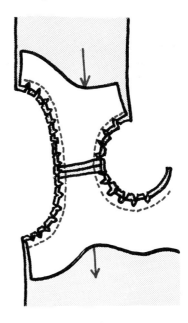

7. Turn the bodice right side out by pulling each **back** piece, through its own shoulder seam, to come out between the garment and facing, at the front. Press the seams at neck and armholes.

8. Now stitch the **back seam** of the bodice.

9. Set the zip, if any, into the neck opening.

10. Slip-stitch the facing in place down the inner sides of the zip (page 35).

37

11. Now stitch the **underarm** seams of the bodice, and straight on up the facing, as one seam.

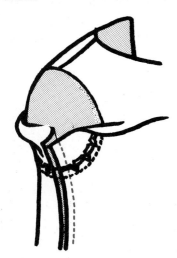

12. Neaten the loose edge of the facing.
13. Turn down the facing inside the armhole; and hold it, with a few stitches, to the bodice underarm seam turnings.

LINING SLEEVES

Without lining the rest of the garment, this is only done:

1. To let the sleeve of an unlined jersey jacket slip on more easily. Use the way shown on page 40.

2. To support a full puffed sleeve. Cut the lining smaller than the sleeve, to fit the arm. First, machine together the lower edges of sleeve and lining—this will be instead of a hem.

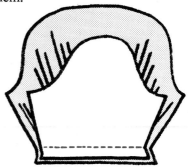

Then stitch the underarm seams of the sleeve and the lining, all as one seam.

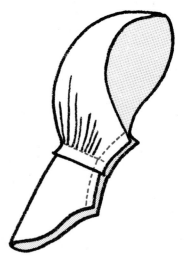

Fold the lining inside, and tack the tops of sleeve and lining, together, into the armhole.

LINING A JACKET

1. Finish the jacket, including the sleeves and hems, and give it a final pressing.

2. Cut the lining to the same pattern as the jacket, not including the width of the facings—but allow a *pleat* of 1″ (2·5 cm) extra down the centre back for ease. Tack this pleat in place, and leave the tacking there until the lining is finished. Hold the top inch of the pleat together with a few cross-stitches; and do the same at the waistline.

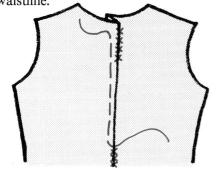

3. Stitch the **darts** and **side seams** of the lining, but not the shoulder seams. Press well now—you will not be able to press the lining once it is set in.

4. Lay the jacket, wrong side up, on the table; lay the lining, right side up, on top of it. Tack them together across the back, from armhole to armhole, to set the lining in its proper place.

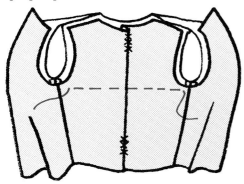

5. Fold the lining fronts out of the way, and tack together the seam turnings of the jacket and lining, from the armhole down to about 4″ (10 cm) from the hem edge. (This tacking will stay in place when the jacket is finished.)

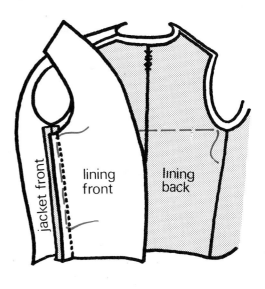

6. Turn in and **pin** the front edges of the lining to the front facings, starting just above the hem edge and working up to bust level.

7. Now turn the jacket inside out; and put it either on a dress form, or over a padded coat-hanger, or better still on a kind friend. Finish pinning the front edges of the lining to the facings, easing them in if you need to, right up to the shoulder seams.

8. Pin the lining armhole to the jacket armhole, with their edges level.

39

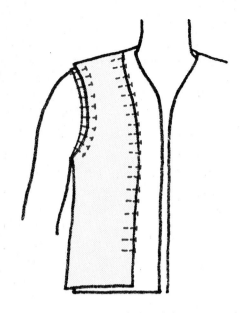

11. Take the jacket off the model. **Slip-stitch** the shoulder seams, then all round the fronts and neck edge, up one side and down the other. Tack round the armholes, through the seam allowances.

12. Take out the tacking across the back, so that the lining hangs free.

13. Crease the **hem**. It should hang $\frac{1}{2}''$ (1·2 cm) **above** the jacket hem. Now push this creased edge another $\frac{1}{2}''-\frac{3}{4}''$ (1·2–2 cm) further up, away from the jacket hem, so that there is at least 1″ (2·5 cm) clear below it. Slip-stitch in place—the extra length of the lining will make a fold giving extra ease, but not showing on the outside. It will form a loose tuck where the hem meets the front facing.

9. Smooth the back of the lining upwards to the collar or back neck facing of the jacket. Turn in and pin the raw edge of the lining along the back of the neck. You will have to clip the curve, to let this turning lie flat.

10. Turn in the back shoulder seam allowance, and pin this folded edge over the front lining, all along the shoulder seam.

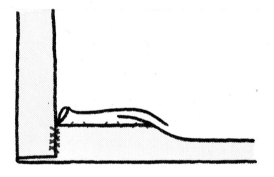

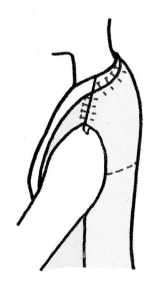

14. Now line the **sleeves.** Stitch the seam of the sleeve lining, but take a smaller turning, to give plenty of room. Press.

15. Turn both the sleeve and sleeve lining **inside out**. Lay them side by side. Match the sleeve seams, and tack their turnings together from the underarm down to 4″ (10 cm) above the wrist.

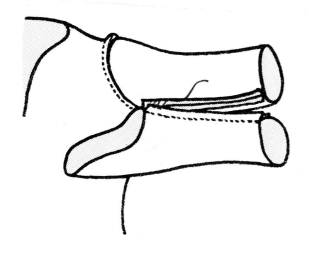

Now that they are joined together on the wrong sides, put your hand down inside the jacket sleeve (as if you were putting it on), catch hold of the wrist ends of sleeve **and lining**, and pull both of them back through to the right side. This gets the lining inside. It is perfectly simple, when you have the garment in your hands.

16. Now turn the sleeve inside out again—this time, the lining will be in its proper place. Turn in its top edge and pin it round the armhole seam. Spread the fullness, so that little gathers or pleats form over the shoulder. Slip-stitch in place.

17. Turn the hem of the sleeve lining (in the same way as the jacket lining), and push it up at least $\frac{1}{2}''$ (1·2 cm) before slip-stitching it.

LINING A COAT

Follow the same steps as for a jacket. The only difference is that the hem of the coat lining is not stitched to the garment, but hangs loose. Hold it in place only with $\frac{1}{2}''$ (1·2 cm) French tacks at the side seams (see page 92).

If there is a back vent to the coat, the lining should have a vent too. They should be slip-stitched together down their sides.

LINING A JACKET OR COAT, EDGE-TO-EDGE

There is a very simple way to do this—entirely by machine. It is useful for thin fabrics, when the lining is about the same weight as the garment—as with plain and patterned cottons.

1. Cut the lining to the same pattern as the coat.

2. Make up the garment and tack any collar in place. A stand-up collar works well with this method. Leave all the edges unfinished—neckline, fronts, hem, and wrist ends of sleeves. Press well—you will not have another chance. Make up the lining, but do not set in its sleeves.

3. Stitch sleeve linings to sleeves round the wrists. Leave the armhole ends of the linings for the moment.

4. Now place jacket and lining **right sides** together. Tack together all the edges, join-

MOUNTING

This is a different way of lining a garment. It is good for keeping skirts in shape, and is also used for fabrics with an open or very loose weave, to stop the seam turnings from showing through, and to give body to the whole garment. Foam-backed materials get their stiffness in the same way, with one layer of fabric "mounted" on another. Use a lining fabric or, for a very stiff effect, a thin Vilene.

1. Cut out all the garment pieces—then cut them out again in the mounting fabric.

2. Make the markings on the mounting fabric only—this can be done with a tracing wheel and dressmaker's carbon paper.

3. Place each lining piece on the wrong side of each garment piece, matching and tacking them together round the edges. Now, keeping the pieces flat, tack along the straight grain, from top to bottom, down the length of the garment. This will keep both layers exactly true, and stop one drooping out of place while you are making up the garment.

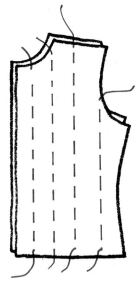

ing jacket to lining round the fronts, neckline and hem, leaving only a 6″ (15 cm) gap in the hem, at the back. Beginning at the back, machine right round as one seam. Trim edges, clip corners and turn the garment right-side-out through the gap. Slip-stitch the sides of this opening. Press all edges lightly.

5. Turn the sleeves inside out. Pin the sleeve linings over the jacket lining at the armholes. Slip-stitch in place.

6. Top-stitching $\frac{3}{8}$″ (1 cm) from all the edges is a good finish, and makes sure that the lining does not roll over and show.

LINING LEATHER OR SUEDE JACKETS

Use the same method to machine the linings into leather garments, where hand sewing is too difficult. The lining is stitched all round to the facings and hem-turnings, which will already be in place.

This is, indeed, the way linings are put into most ready-made clothes today.

You will need three or four lines of tacking down each piece. This is a slow job—but there is no point in mounting at all unless it is well done. If you can use machine-basting instead of hand tacking, the work will not take so long.

4. Now treat both layers as a single piece of fabric, and make up the garment as usual. It helps to tack through the centres of all dart markings—this makes it easier to fold the double fabric evenly to make the dart.

5. Neaten both layers **together** in seam turnings. Take out the tackings when you are ready to turn up the hem.

6. Stitch the hem to the mounting fabric **only**, not right through to the outside. It will not show at all.

7. Do **not** try to mount jersey fabrics. It is almost impossible to match just the same amount of stretch in the mounting fabric, so the result can look "bubbly" all over.

5 MANAGING YOUR FABRICS

Few fabrics are really difficult to manage if you learn how they need to be handled, and prepare them carefully for sewing.

CHECKED FABRICS

Success comes from **matching the checks** and **planning the layout** BEFORE cutting out.

Checks can be **even** (the same either way up);

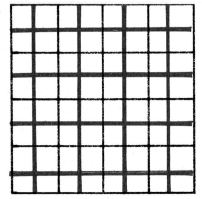

or **uneven**, and need a **with-nap** layout (page 55);

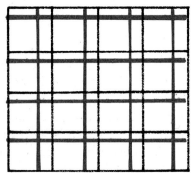

Usually, a thick downward stripe and a thick sideways stripe show up as the strongest part of the pattern—these are the lines to match.

Placing your checks   Hold the fabric against you and try the effect in a mirror. A strong downward line may look best at the centre front (with a V-neck, for example), or the space between the lines may look better at the centre. A strong sideways line usually looks best if it crosses the bodice about 3″ (8 cm) below the point of the shoulder, level with the dot on the pattern at the armhole seamline.

Preparing your fabric   To make sure that the checks will match on both sides of your garment, fold the material in half, selvedges together. Unless the checks go through to the wrong side, fold with the right side **out** so that you can see them while pinning. Work on a large table or a carpeted floor—the floor is much easier if you can keep away cats, dogs and interested children.

Pin the material together every 6″ (15 cm) or so, near the **selvedges**, matching and pinning through the centres of the main checks. Now pin along near the **fold** of your fabric—this will come either on a check-line or exactly half-way between two lines. You must be accurate here, as you may need to have your centre front or back on this fold. Now pin **each end** of the fabric, from selvedges to fold, matching checks as you go. There should be no wrinkles any-

44

where. Lastly, pin here and there across the fabric, through the centres of a few checks—the pins should come out at the centres of checks on the underneath layer.

Take plenty of time over this, as a perfect match means that your right and left sides, cut from the double thickness, are sure to be checked alike.

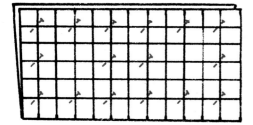

HOW TO MATCH CHECKS

1. **The front** Lay the centre front of the pattern piece on the main downward check-line, or half-way between two lines. If the centre line on the pattern is a fold-line, place this on the fold of the material. Move the pattern up or down along the fold until the strongest sideways check-line comes level with the dot on the armhole seam. **Make certain that the straight grain arrow is exactly parallel to the checks,** or they will slope down on one side.

2. **The Back** Lay out the pattern piece in the same way as the front. If you are having a main check-line at the centre front, then you should also have one at the centre back.

3. **Side seams of the bodice** The checks on the back and front bodice should be level at the notches **below** any underarm dart. (See next diagram.)

4. **Darts** at the shoulder or waist look best if they are centred on a check, or half-way between checks. Mark them as usual; but when you pin them up, keep an eye on the right side, as you may have to move them just a little to where they look right. Make sure that darts below the bust come to just below **your** bust, to make a smooth line. Darts above and below the waist should match together at the waistline.

5. **Sleeves** Lay the pattern so that the main downward line runs through the mark at the head of the sleeve—and then goes parallel to the straight grain arrow. The main sideways line should go through the dot at the front edge of the armhole, so that it matches the same line on the bodice.

45

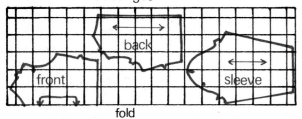

selvedges

back

front   sleeve

fold

6. **The Collar**   Make sure the checks of the collar and garment match at the centre back. If you cut the centre back of the garment on a fold, then place the collar also on the fold. This will make the checks at both **ends** of the collar match, too.

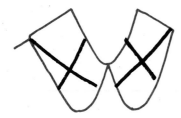

7. **The Facings**   Cut the facings so that the revers of a jacket will carry on one downward check-line from the collar.

The **sideways** lines on the facings should match the sideways lines of the jacket front.

8. **Skirt and trousers**   Use the balance marks on the side seams to match the sideways check-lines. On **trousers**, the fronts (and backs) are bound to match each other at centre seams, if they have been cut from the carefully matched double thickness of fabric. On a **skirt,** put a check-line down the centre front if there is one down the centre front of the bodice or jacket.

The downward check-lines at the side seams will make neat arrow-points on a flared skirt, if they are cut like this to come into the seam at the same level.

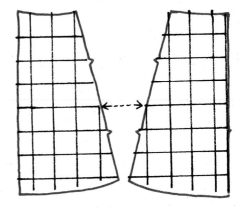

9. **The whole layout**   Arrange your large pattern pieces on the fabric first, as close together as they will go, always matching the dots or balance marks to the lines of the check as you want them. **Remember the straight grain arrow must always run parallel to the check-lines.** If you have an **uneven** check use a with-nap layout, keeping the tops of the pattern pieces all pointing the same way.

Fit the smaller pieces on to the rest of the material; do not try to match checks on inside facings that will not show.

10. **Using checks on the bias for contrast** Yokes, sleeves, patch pockets, facings or bound buttonholes can all look well on the

46

bias, with the rest of the garment on the straight grain.

Very large checks are not usually quite square, and will not easily match up—but sleeves cut on the bias can look stunning if you match their diagonal checks with the bodice check-lines, just below the shoulder.

11. **Extra fabric for matching checks**   Allow $\frac{1}{4}$ yard (23 cm) extra for checks up to 4″ (10 cm) across. Checks smaller than 2″ (5 cm) will need only $\frac{1}{8}$ yard (11 cm) extra; checks smaller than $\frac{1}{4}$″ (6 mm) need no extra fabric as they are not usually matched at all.

12. **Stitching checks on thick fabrics** can safely be done over pins **set at right angles** to the seamline. (See pin-basting, page 15). They will hold the checks in place, and the machine needle will pass over them if you machine slowly. This does not work so well on thin fabrics, where it is better to baste.

13. **Slip-basting checks**   Matching is easier when you work from the right side. Fold both seam allowances to the inside and slip-baste on the **outside** along the seam-line, taking a stitch first in one fold and then in the other. Turn to the wrong side and machine over the basting.

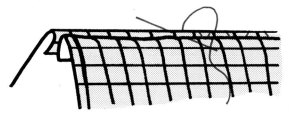

Striped fabrics are matched in the same way as checked ones, but are easier to manage as they need to be matched in one direction only. Narrow stripes should not need any extra fabric.

CORDUROY

This has a ribbed pile and is usually made up with the rib (and the pile) running downwards; but yokes, cuffs and pockets can look well with the rib going sideways for contrast. Use a **with-nap** layout (page 55) for cutting out.

Corduroy can be machine-washed and drip-dried. Before it is quite dry, brush it hard, first against the pile and then with it. It should not need pressing, but seams can be touched up with the tip of the iron.

As well as stretchable knits, some woven fabrics can drop out of shape. Crêpe is one, if it is not bonded on a backing. Avoid styles that have wide skirts cut on the cross—these will drop unevenly. Choose instead skirts cut on the straight grain, with unpressed pleats for fullness—to show off the pretty softness of crêpe without risking a droopy hem.

If you **must** make a circular skirt of crêpe, finish the waistline and hang it by the waist for a **week**, to stretch and drop out. Try it on and get a friend to chalk a level round the hemline. For a curved edge, it is best to use a narrow hem, so trim off to a 1″ (2·5 cm) turning, and finish with bias binding or two rows of machine stitching close to the edge.

Knitted fabrics are comfortable and easy to wear, as they stretch with every movement but spring back into shape again. Some stretch more than others, but these points are useful for all knit fabrics;

1. Knits come in widths up to 70″ (177 cm), so check the length you need to buy—it may be less than you expect.

2. Knits are best treated as napped fabrics (page 55) as most show a little change of shade the other way up.

3. Cutting out must be done with the straight grain arrow parallel to the rib of the knit—the "wale"—which is like the grain of a woven fabric. (If the wale of a *bonded* knit is off-true, there is nothing you can do about it, so watch for this when you buy. It is better to keep the arrow along the **wale** than parallel to the edge of the fabric.)

4. Do not place main pattern pieces across the crease down the centre of jersey fabrics —this crease often cannot be pressed out.

5. Use polyester thread to give stretch to the seams, and a small machine stitch—about 12 to the inch (5 to the cm). A very narrow zig-zag stitch is useful for seams; fully-automatic machines have a built-in back-stitch, which also helps to keep the stretch. Special ball-point machine needles make for smoother sewing of knitted fabrics.

6. Because knits stretch so well, they also stretch where they should not. So **tape** shoulder seams and sew **bias binding** round armholes (page 16).

7. Seam edges that curl can be helped to lie flat by stitching along each edge with a wide 3-step zig-zag. Otherwise, if your knit

fabric does not unravel, you will not need to neaten.

8. For **lining** knits, choose a knitted lining fabric, such as nylon tricot, so as not to spoil the stretch of the garment. Use a **stretch** interfacing such as Knitted Staflex (page 31).

9. **Hems** should be catch-stitched (page 83) after zig-zag stitching the raw edge. Bias binding is also a good finish if the fabric is not a **very** stretchable knit.

10. If you need to press do it on the wrong side, lightly, so that the material is not flattened.

Jerseys bonded to a backing material   These are the firmest of the knits, with very little stretch. They are usually made of wool or acrylic (Courtelle, Acrilan, Orlon). They are very easy to sew, and save time and money as their lining is built-in. Even interfacing may not be needed.

Double jerseys and warp-knits can be thick or thin, and made of any fibre. They stretch more sideways than the bonded jerseys, but very little up-and-down. The thicker ones are useful for skirts and trousers; and the thinner ones, such as tricot, for blouses, shirts and underwear. **Raschel Warp-knit** is a very firm fabric, even when it is open and lacy, and springs back to the same shape after washing.

Stretchable knits, which can be stretched up to nearly double their width, are usually made of single jersey, like hand knitting. They can be in wool, cotton or any of the man-made fibres. They must be made up **quite differently** from ordinary fabrics, as they stretch enough to mould themselves to the body, without any darts or shaping at the bust or hip.

1. Choose the special patterns marked "Designed for Stretch Knits Only"; but **do** cut them with at least 1″ (2·5 cm) seam allowances at all side edges, because they may be a tighter fit than you like. They show up every tiny bulge—so, unless your figure has curves in the right places only, you may want to wear your stretch-knit dress a little looser.

2. To fit, tack up the side seams and hold the loose, lower ends of the tacking threads firm by winding them round pins. Put the garment on a hanger overnight; then try it on and check that the side seams are not pulled up too tightly. Finish off the tacking at the right tightness; and then stitch up the seams, stretching them slightly as you sew. This will avoid the ripple effect that an over-stretched seam can show, or the looped-up look of one sewn too tightly.

3. Sew with polyester thread and a zig-zag stitch about $\frac{1}{8}$″ (3 mm) wide and 12–14 stitches to the inch (6 to the cm). Or use a 3-step zig-zag. Either will give all the stretch needed.

4. Do not lose the soft, stretchy look of the fabric by firming it up with interfacings. Try not to use facings either, as these knits can roll over badly. Instead, bind the edges with the fabric itself, cut in strips straight across the wale—the way that knits stretch most.

5. Fasten with rouleau loops (page 90), ties or lacings, instead of buttonholes which might pull out of shape.

6. Do not line stretchable jersey—instead, wear a plain, well-fitting slip, or just bra, briefs and tights, under it.

49

LACE

Dress lace is no more difficult to handle than any other fabric; but take care not to let hems and seam edges show through, as they would spoil the pattern of the lace. A **false hem** (page 83), turned up with net, will keep the pattern clear at the hemline—or you can use the scalloped edge of lace flouncing as the hem edge of a skirt or sleeve. For this, place the hem fold-line of the pattern piece **right on** the scalloped edge of the lace, and do not turn up any hem at all.

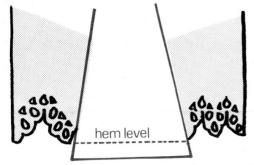

To **neaten seams,** machine the edges together with a straight or zig-zag stitch, $\frac{1}{4}''$ (6 mm) from the seamline, and trim closely. Use a short presser foot with a turned-up toe (a quilting or cording foot), so that the toe will not catch in the lace.

Skirt seams can be matched to the pattern of the lace by laying one edge over the other, right sides up, and working zig-zag machine stitch in a line following the pattern of the lace.

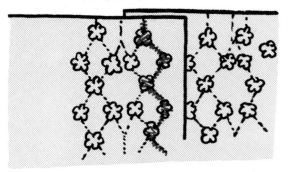

Trim off the loose edges on both sides and the seam will not show at all. Give yourself plenty of seam allowance to work with.

Never **fit** lace closely—it is not built to hold you in, and will wrinkle up or tear if you make it too tight. Bodices can be mounted onto a stronger fabric (page 42).

For sewing **lace edging** to other fabrics, tack the edge of the lace in place on the right side of the other fabric, and stitch with a machine satin-stitch (a medium-wide zig-zag, with the stitches very close together), following the edge of the lace. Trim off the raw edge on the wrong side, close to the satin-stitch. This stitch looks best if you work it in a machine embroidery thread.

Press lace on the wrong side over a piece of soft blanket, so that the raised threads of the pattern are not flattened.

LEATHER, SUÈDE AND FAKE LEATHERS

Leathers make splendid garments of great style. They are not too difficult to handle if simple, un-fussy patterns are used. Remember that the whole garment has to be machine-stitched, as hand-sewing is very hard and not very strong.

Raglan sleeves are better than set-in ones, because they have straighter seams—and also because they give more room, as most leathers will not ease or stretch. Sleeveless styles are good—so are 4 or 6 panelled skirts.

Leather trousers can be hot and stiff to wear—they also take up a great deal of leather—but wash-leather ones are possible, with a seam at knee level.

Making a calico model   Leather is far too expensive to take chances with, or to risk a disaster. It must be cut exactly right the first time, with no question of taking out any stitching or altering any seams.

The only safe way to do this is to make up the whole garment first, in a cheap material, to see how it fits you. Then, any alterations can be made to the pattern, before cutting your leather. Unbleached calico is the best fabric to use for the model; it is very cheap, stiff enough to behave like leather—and you can always tie-dye or paint it when you have finished, to use as a fun-garment later.

When you are **fitting the model**, make sure you mark exactly the placing of buttons, button-holes and pockets. Check also the length of the garment. Let the sleeves be $\frac{1}{2}''$ (1·2 cm) longer than usual, to allow for the elbow creases that always settle into leather during wear. Your hems need not be more than $1\frac{1}{2}''$ (4 cm) deep;

so if you are sure of the length now, you may save yourself buying more leather than you really need. But do allow plenty of room round the body—leather should not be fitted closely.

Real leathers are bought as whole skins; or as side, back or belly pieces.

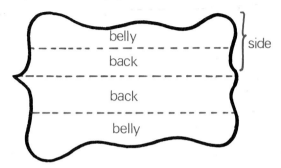

The belly is thinner and not as strong, but much cheaper. It is useful for accessories and smaller garments.

Take your pattern with you when you buy leather, to make sure it will fit on the skin—there may be holes or bad patches to avoid. Leather is much cheaper in markets than in shops, but be sure to check its quality.

You might use less leather by putting in an extra seam, such as a yoke, to make your pattern pieces smaller and easier to fit on the skin. Keep all your scraps for squared-up or crazy patchwork—or for motifs to stitch on other garments.

Seams on leather are best overlaid and double-stitched. Trim off one seam allowance and place this cut edge on the stitching line of the other piece, right sides up. Stitch near the edge.

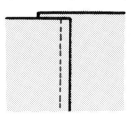

51

Then turn over and stitch near the other edge on the wrong side.

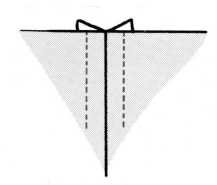

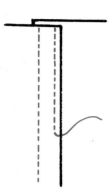

Vinyl and fake leathers are sold from the roll and cut out like fabric, with an ordinary pattern layout. The cut edges of fake leathers are cheap-looking, so use plain open seams that will not show the raw edges.

Suède and mock-suède, softer than leather, can be made into more supple garments. They look well with knitted sleeves and collars, or teamed with tweed. Suède picks up dirt very easily, so buy the washable kind. A special suède brush, or rubber, also helps to keep it clean.

Wash-leather (Chamois leather) is the easiest to handle, and the cheapest, of all the natural skins. If you have never tried leather before this is where to begin. It gathers beautifully (by machine) into cuffs and yokes, and moulds easily to the figure. A whole large skin is up to 27″ (69 cm) long, so jackets with long sleeves can easily be made from six skins (two each for back, fronts, and sleeves). Skirts, even below the knee, use only four.

A good seam for wash-leather is a top-stitched one.

As washleather stretches, it is as well to sew tape into the shoulder and armhole seams—and into the cuffs of gathered sleeves.

Of course, it washes beautifully; and there is no dye to run or fade. Wash it with glove shampoo. Dry flat on a towel and, just before the garment is quite dry, rub it between your hands and pull it gently to soften the skins again.

Cutting out   The grain of leather goes from the animal's head to its tail. Place your main pattern pieces along this grain, and the garment will keep its shape. Put the pieces on the wrong side of the skin and hold them down with kitchen weights, or large pebbles, instead of pins. Pin-holes might show, and would weaken the leather—pins are almost impossible to push in anyway.

Draw round the pieces with a felt-tip pen. Check that you have turned over the pattern, when placing the right and left sides—otherwise you may find yourself with part of the garment cut from the wrong side of the skin. (It is not, of course, possible to cut leather as a double thickness.)

Sharp shears will cut most leathers—a knife or razor blade is not so easy to control. Instead of tacking, hold the pieces together with hair-grips—or better still, hair clips.

Making up

Machining Set a very long machine stitch, 6 or 7 to the inch (3 to the cm), and use buttonhole twist (such as Gütermann Hela) for strength. Lighten the pressure on the machine foot, so that the leather slides through easily. A little talcum powder rubbed on vinyl, or shiny patent leathers, will stop them from sticking in the machine. This will not hurt the machine.

Flattening edges You cannot iron leather or fake-leather, so this is how to make the edges of open seams, or cut-open darts, lie flat. On the wrong side, cover the seam edges with a cloth or brown paper, and hammer them down with a wooden mallet. Then stick them flat with rubber glue, such as Copydex. This will stand either washing or dry cleaning. For accessories, such as bags, that will not be washed or dry cleaned, stick down the edges with double-sided Sellotape—it is quicker, easier and a lot less messy to use.

Collar edges and hem turnings should be turned to the wrong side, notched if they are curved, hammered, and stuck down just along the crease. Collars can be top-stitched on the right side.

Front edges look best with a "shirt" finish; cut without seam turnings, and faced on the **right** side with a 2″–3″ (5–8 cm) strip of leather. Stick it in place along the front,

right sides up, and top-stitch along both edges.

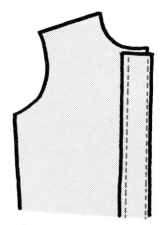

Zips can be set in quite easily. Trim off the seam allowances of the opening, and use double-sided Sellotape to stick the zipper tapes, separately, to the wrong sides of the opening edges. Then stitch each side as usual.

Buttonholes, too, are simple. On the right side, through both the garment and the facing, stitch the shape of the buttonhole, $\frac{1}{4}''$ (6 mm) longer than the button, and about $\frac{3}{8}''$ (1 cm) wide.

Use a seam-ripper or razor-blade, and cut from each end to the middle, through the double thickness.

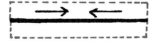

Each button should have a small flat button sewn beneath it on the wrong side, to take the strain from the leather; sew both buttons on together, taking the thread from the top button right through the underneath one. Large, hammered-on snaps are another good finish on leather.

Linings should be made up complete, and then sewn in by machine, as shown on page 42.

Leather or suède patchwork is simple to do and stunning to wear. The *squared-up* kind is made by stitching together squares of leather to make long strips. Then stitch the strips together, side by side. Use overlaid seams, to keep the patchwork flat.

Crazy patchwork needs a backing—hessian is good; stick on it, with double-sided Sellotape, scraps of leather or suède of different shapes and colours to make any pattern or picture you fancy. Then top-stitch. Make tote-bags like this.

MAN-MADE FIBRES

These are a joy to sew and wear, as they keep their shape beautifully and do not shrink or crease—but you cannot shape or pleat them by steam.

Shaping is best done by careful and accurate tacking of seams and darts. Try on the garment and make sure **before** machining that there will be no wrinkles and that the fit is right. Use a polyester thread, such as Trylko (coarse), Drima (medium), or Gütermann Mara (fine), on **all** man-made fibres. Cotton threads are not strong or stretchy enough.

Pleats can be heat-set in the factory, but some fibres will not pleat well with an iron at home. Before you reach the right heat, the fabric may be damaged. Acrylic, nylon and polyester are best edge-stitched $\frac{1}{8}''$ (3 mm) away from the front and back edges of the pleats; especially on jersey fabrics. This makes sharp and lasting pleats that will drip-dry back into place.

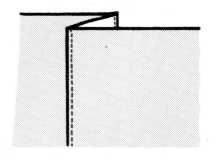

in one garment is new in dressmaking. Each kind of material used to be made up on its own. Now it is quite usual to mix thick and thin fabrics—woven, jersey and leather—whatever looks well together, goes together. The rules for success are simple;

1. If a heavier fabric is used for the skirt than for the bodice of a dress, then give it some support at the waist. Sew a tape into the waist seam, or fit a petersham ribbon inside the waistline (page 93) to take the weight.

2. When sewing jersey to a woven fabric, make sure the jersey is basted evenly, and stretched the right amount to make a good fit. Hold it firmly pulled out as you machine. These seams can be lumpy if the jersey is unevenly stretched.

3. Mix fabrics **only** to show off their differences. Do not make jersey "pretend" to be like a woven material—use it for the part of the garment that needs to be stretchy. Eye-catching outfits can be made from different fabrics, such as cotton jersey and woven cotton, printed with the same pattern.

4. Be sure that the fabrics you mix can all be washed in the same way; if not, they must be washed or cleaned in the way that suits the most delicate of the fabrics.

These feel rough when you stroke them one way (against the nap), and smooth the other way (with the nap). When the nap runs downwards, the cloth will look a lighter colour—when it runs upwards the colour will seem darker. All the pieces must be cut out to stroke smoothly **in the same direction**, or you will get a patchy-looking garment. Use the with-nap pattern layout shown on your pattern instruction sheet, with the tops of all the pattern pieces lying towards one end of your fabric.

Fake fur usually has a long pile, and should be made up with the nap running downwards. When sewing fake fur, it is best to pin-baste fairly closely, and machine straight over the pins (page 15). Use a ruler, or the blades of your dressmaking shears, to stroke the fur away from the cut edges, between the two layers; then after the seam is stitched, you should not need to winkle out any tufts of fur caught in the stitching. Trim all the pile off the seam turnings, and press with the very tip of the iron to flatten the seams.

A one-way print also counts as a nap, and must be cut so that it comes the right way up when you wear it, like this;

Not like this;

See also Velvet, page 58.

REVERSIBLE FABRICS

Some of these are really two separate fabrics, held together by thin threads that can easily be unravelled at the cut edges. They are often checked on one side and plain on the other, and are useful for making reversible unlined coats.

Seams are neatest if the two thicknesses of the fabric are pulled apart for about 2″ (5 cm) along the edges to be joined. Place right sides together and stitch *the right side layers only*.

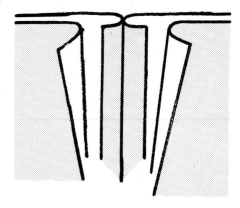

Then turn in the **wrong-side** edges to meet each other and slip-stitch them together on the inside of the garment.

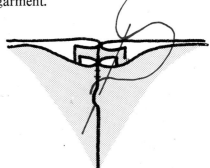

Hems, collars and front edges are best finished by binding with woollen braid.

Seams on fabrics like chiffon and voile can be seen from the outside, so the neatest ones to use are very narrow French seams. Stay-stitch all bias edges at shoulders and armholes, as sheers can stretch and fray badly. Use a fine polyester thread, such as Drima or Mara.

Bias binding, made of crossway strips cut from the fabric, is a good finish for necklines, armholes and collar edges; because facings would show through.

Hems need to be deep, to give weight at the lower edge of the garment. A 6″ (15 cm) hem on a straight, full skirt is not too deep; make sure that the lay of the hem (the first turning-in) goes down the whole depth, so that no ragged edge can show through.

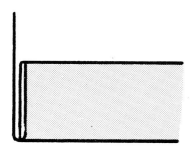

Avoid **buttonholes** in sheer fabrics—instead, use rouleau loops (page 90). **Gathers** look beautiful on sheers; so look for frills, flounces, or gathers into cuffs, when choosing your pattern.

is bulky; so the best seam to use is an overlaid one, made without a turning. Trim off one seam allowance and lay this edge against the stitching line of the other piece, right sides up. Stitch right over the raw edge with a wide zig-zag stitch (or better still a 3-step zig-zag if your machine can do it).

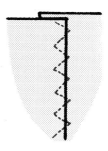

Turn over to the wrong side and stitch down the other raw edge in the same way. This seam almost disappears into the fabric, and the edges cannot unravel.

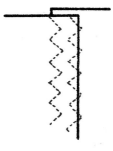

Zips can be set into towelling quite safely if the material is turned in **well clear** of the zipper teeth. Use the ordinary machine presser foot (not the zipper one) so that you can sew a zig-zag stitch. Or back-stitch the zip in by hand. Zips with wide tapes in a contrasting colour look well on towelling sportswear.

Hems can be turned up in a single fold, and stitched with a 3-step zig-zag.

VELVET

has a nap, so it must be cut with the tops of all the pattern pieces pointing the same way. It looks best if the pile runs upwards, as the colour will seem deeper and richer. Panne velvet (with a flat, shiny pile) and stretch velvet (for trousers and tight-fitting garments) look best and most shiny if the pile runs downwards. Brush them well the way of the pile. **Cutting out** can be difficult, because velvet's deep pile "creeps" when right sides are placed together. It is safer to cut out in a single thickness. Make sure that you **turn the pattern over** before cutting the second half of the bodice, skirt etc, or you may find yourself with two left sides.

Pinning and basting should be at right angles to the stitching line, to stop slipping. Pin within the seam allowance, just up to the stitching line, so that any pin marks will not show. Slightly lighten the pressure on the machine foot when stitching. Put in zips by hand. Avoid top-stitching as it squashes the pile and looks messy. Neaten seam edges with a zig-zag stitch or by overcasting.

Ironing would spoil velvet: steaming is the best way to lift out creases. Put the garment on a hanger and move it about in front of the spout of a boiling kettle—or hang it over a hot bath. Seam edges can be flattened by placing the seam, right side down, on the bristle side of a clothes brush, and touching the seamline **only** with the tip of a steam iron.

Washing Most velvets these days can be hand-washed and drip-dried on a hanger. Tricel-and-nylon velvet washes beautifully and dries in an hour. Rayon-and-cotton or all-rayon velvets take longer. When dry, steam out any creased patches. Real silk velvets should not be washed, but can be dry-cleaned.

WOOLLENS

Seams should be neatened by zig-zag machining or by overcasting. Never turn seam edges over into a double thickness, as this makes a bulky seam. On thick woollens it is also important to trim down the edges, especially where seams cross each other.

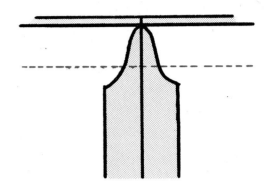

Do not let seams make a shiny mark on the right side of the garment when you press—put a thin card, such as a clean postcard, under the seam edge, and press on the wrong side over the card.

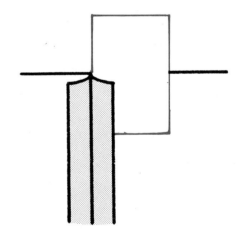

Hems are best finished with seam-binding on straight skirts; bias binding on flared skirts; or by folding back the tacked edge of the hem and catch-stitching the inside of it to the garment. (page 83). Whichever way you use, the hem must be turned up in a single thickness **only**, to avoid bulk. Do not press over the stitched edge of a hem, in case it marks the right side. It is quite safe to cover the hem with a damp cloth and hold your iron **just above but not touching it**, so that the steam can do the work without any pressing.

Shaping   As steam shrinks wool, you can use it to settle down cut-open darts; or to shape a flared hem or the head of a sleeve, into a smooth curve. Put a tailor's pad, or a firmly-rolled towel, under the part to be shrunk, and a damp cloth on top—or use a steam iron. Press with the iron set at No. 2 (warm) to shrink out wrinkles and shape the garment as you wish. Lift off the pressing cloth and let the wool cool before you move it. This will let the shape set.

Pleating   First, tack the pleats in place. Press on a firm ironing board under a damp cloth. Lift off the cloth and **beat in** the pleats with a smooth piece of wood such as the back of a clothes brush. Beat **hard**. This is called "noisy pressing"—it is, but it works. Do not move the garment until the pleats have cooled and set. You may need to touch up the pleat edges after you have taken out the tacking.

6 FASHION AND A FINE FINISH

One reason for making your own clothes is that you can choose exactly the fashion details you want—the size of pocket—the shape of collar —the contrasting fabrics, stitching or trim-mings. When you **buy** a dress, you look for one as near as possible to the picture, in your mind, of what you want. When you **make** a dress, you make it just as you imagine it, right for **you**.

Many ways of making a garment personal and different, which are used by fashion houses, are simple to copy or adapt for your own clothes. This chapter should give you some ideas.

DECORATIVE SEAMS

Channel seam—a bold detail for thick, firm fabrics.

1. With right sides together, machine-baste (largest possible stitch) along the seamline. Press the seam edges open.

2. With wrong sides upwards, cover the seam with a straight-grain strip of fabric—in a

contrasting colour if you like. It should be as wide as the two seam turnings. Baste through all thicknesses.

3. On the right side, top-stitch on each side of the seam, about $\frac{3}{8}''$ (1 cm) away from it. This looks best in a buttonhole twist, using a long machine stitch.

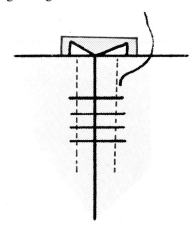

4. Take out the basting and machine basting; the two edges will pull apart a little, just showing the material behind them. Neaten the raw edges on the wrong side.

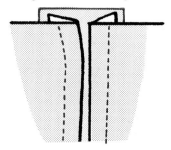

Strap seam—useful for contrasting braid. This is made like a channel seam, except that the strap is put on the **outside**.

1. With **wrong** sides together, machine-stitch the seam. Press the edges open on the right side, and trim them to about $\frac{3}{8}''$ (1 cm) wide.

2. With right sides up, lay a braid over the seam, so that it overlaps the raw edges. Machine close to each edge of the braid. No neatening is needed. This is a good finish for unlined jackets.

Overlaid seams—all those top-stitched from the right side. They are used on yokes, or where there are curves or corners in the seam.

1. Fold under the seam allowance of the top piece, clipping the turning to make it lie flat. Press. Mark the seamline on the lower piece.

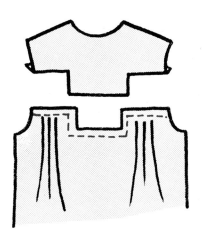

2. Tack together, right sides up, matching the folded edge to the marked seamline. Stitch $\frac{1}{8}''$ (3 mm) from the fold, using buttonhole twist and a long machine stitch for a bold finish.

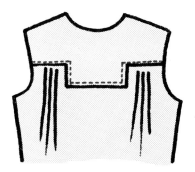

3. Overlaid seams can also be used for piping—putting a folded strip of binding or braid between the two layers.

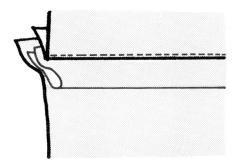

Or to attach a frill, or lace, perhaps down the fronts of a blouse.

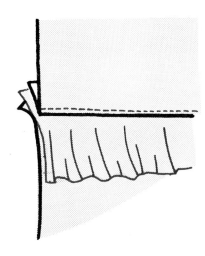

61

Another kind of overlaid seam, used in tailored collars, is done completely by hand (pages 97–8).

Point de Paris or pin-stitched seam For blouses or underwear in fine fabrics, Point de Paris (Paris Stitch) can hold a seam instead of machining. It is an embroidery stitch, like hem-stitching, but does not have to be worked on the straight grain. Use it also for appliqué—stitching on motifs. Use a large-eyed needle and pull up the stitches tightly, to make little holes.

1. Bring up the needle at the edge of the double thickness. Take the first stitch from right to left, through the single thickness.

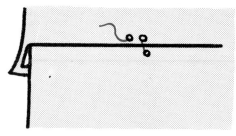

2. Then take the next stitch back and diagonally downwards, through both thicknesses.

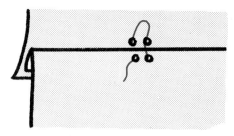

3. Repeat these two stitches all along the seamline.

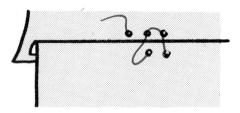

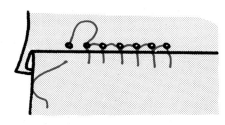

4. You can use this stitch for hems also; then the other side becomes the right side.

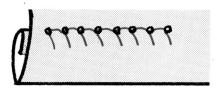

Insertion seam—for thin materials, especially for using with lace.

1. **With straight machining** Press under a seam turning along each edge of fabric. Lay these folded edges so that they just overlap the edges of the lace. Tack and top-stitch along both folds.

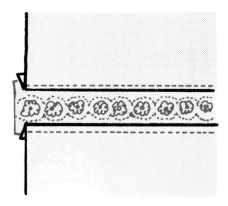

2. **With machine satin-stitch** Tack the edges of the lace **over** the raw edges of both pieces of material. Work close machine satin-stitch right over the edges of the lace. On the wrong side, trim off the raw edges close to the satin-stitch. This finish looks best if you use a machine embroidery thread.

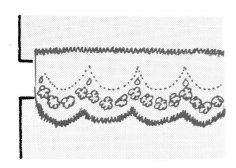

Mantua maker's seam At the time when King Charles II came back from exile in France, bringing all the new French fashions with him, "mantua-makers" were the fashionable dressmakers. They must have worked at a great pace, because this seam is both stitched and neatened at the same time. It is a good "lazy" way to set gathers into a yoke, or to attach a flounce or frill.

1. Tack the edges, right sides together, along the stitching line. Trim the lower edge (or the gathered one) to $\frac{3}{8}''$ (1 cm).

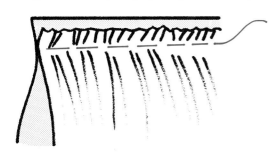

2. Fold the wider edge over the narrower one.

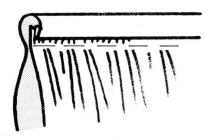

3. Then fold over *both* the edges together, so that they meet the tacking.

4. Machine-stitch right over the tacking, through all the thicknesses.

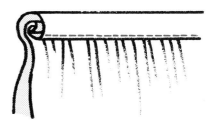

5. The finished seam—right side.

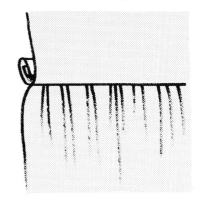

PLEATS

On paper patterns, the pleating lines are marked in pairs.

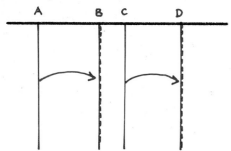

One line has to be creased and moved over to meet the next one, to make the pleat.

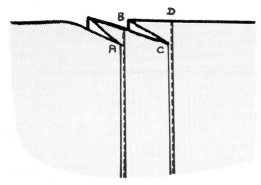

For pleats to hang well, these lines must be marked **exactly**. Use tailor's tacks (page 14). It helps to have two colours of thread, one for the "pleat" line and the other for the "meet" line. Make your tacks from the top to the bottom of each pleat line, every few inches. If the pleats are to be stitched part of the way down, mark in another colour where the stitching is to end.

Fold the pleats over carefully, along the marks, and tack them all the way. Press them in place down to 6″ (15 cm) from the lower edge. Do not press pleats below this, until you have turned up the hem. The pleated sections should hang smooth and unwrinkled when you hold them against yourself—try this, and get the line of each section right **before** seaming the garment together.

If a seam comes at the inside turn of a pleat, clip its seam edges right back to the seam stitching, level with the top of the hem, and overcast the raw edge. This will let the back of the pleat lie flat.

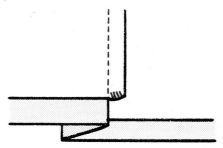

Inside the hem, trim and press open the seam turnings, to avoid bulk.

Try not to alter the placing of pleats. It is better to make any alterations at the side seams, or wherever there is no pleat. The exception is with tartans or any large checks; then, try to get the main line of the check showing at the same place in each pleat. This might mean spacing the pleats further apart or nearer together—even then, alter the pattern as little as possible.

If a group of pleats hangs open badly, it may be because their inside edges have been cut back to avoid bulk.

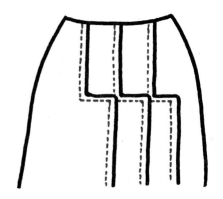

The cure for this is to put a thin lining in, to support the pleats above the cut-away part. The sides of the lining will be taken into the side seams.

GODETS

Godets look like pleats, but are really triangles of fabric let into a straight seam, such as a skirt seam. They can give as much extra room for movement as pleats, without so much bulk.

1. Stitch the seam above the opening for the godet, up to the waistline. Press the edges open all the way.

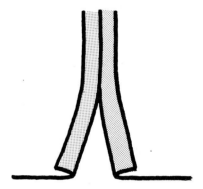

2. Now seam one side of the godet triangle, from the point to the base, to each side of the opening. Do this in two separate seams.

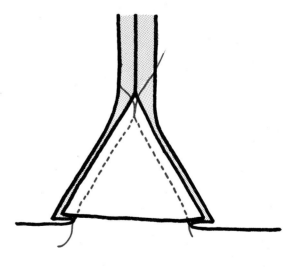

3. Press creases in the godet so that the two seams meet at the centre; looking, on the right side, like an inverted pleat,

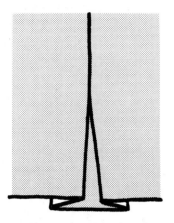

and on the wrong side like this;

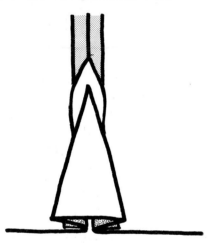

4. Or leave the godet uncreased for a flared look—useful for flared trousers.

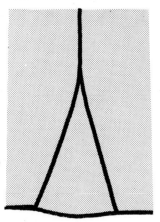

COLLARS

No part of a garment shows more than the collar—so it is extra important to make and attach it perfectly. Collars can also be a give-away of your skill, as faults of fitting and stitching show up so clearly.

Here are a few kinds of collar, with the easier ones first.

Bound collar   This is simple because it can be made from only one thickness of fabric. Bind the edge with a bias strip (a different colour looks well), or with ready-made bias binding. Stitch it first to the right side, easing the binding round the curves.

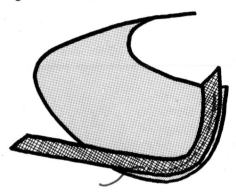

Now turn to the wrong side, fold in the edge of the bias, and hem just inside the first stitching.

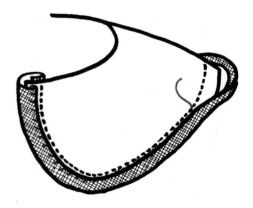

This is a good collar for children's clothes or casual wear, as it is easy to wash and iron.

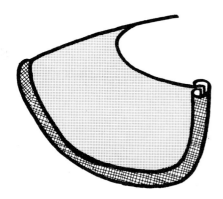

Piped collar Collars made from a double thickness of fabric can be given interest by piping—perhaps in a contrasting fabric, such as satin piping round a wool collar.

1. Fold a bias strip—about 1½″ (4 cm) wide —with wrong sides together. Match the raw edges of the strip to the outer edge of one collar piece, and tack. Make sure there is plenty of ease in the bias strip; then it will lie flat when the collar is turned right side out.

2. Now lay the other collar piece on top, so that the piping is between the two thick-nesses of collar. Stitch round the outer edge.

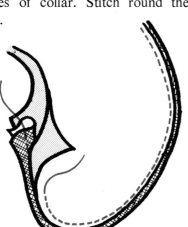

3. Layer and clip the edges, and turn the collar right side out through the neckline edges. If you would like the piping to look fatter, thread through it some thick, soft yarn, such as nylon double-knitting. (Not wool, because of shrinking.) This is simpler than using piping cord, and gives a softer finish.

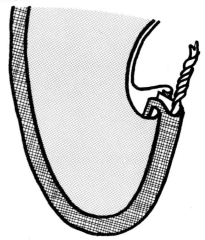

Shirt collar with a separate stand The "stand" of a collar is the interfaced band that stands up from the neckline. The collar turns down from the top of the stand. These collars set best if they are cut in two parts;

The Neckband, an almost straight piece, to stand up.

The Collar, much more curved, to lie wider on the shoulders.

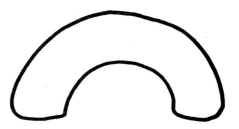

Stitch each collar piece to its interfaced band, and press the seams open.

Place the collars with right sides together. Stitch the **ends** of the bands and all round the collar pieces.

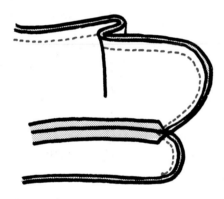

Trim, turn and press. The finished collar will look like this;

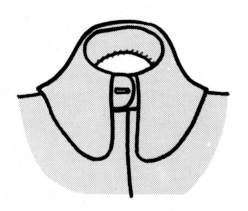

Pressing collars   The seam round the collar edge should be pressed *just* to the under-side, where it will not show in wear. This is the easiest way;

1. Turn the collar through to the right side.
2. Roll the seam between finger and thumb to exactly the position you want it.
3. Tack and press it just a millimetre out of sight on the underneath layer.

Attaching collars can be done in two main ways;

1. **With facings**   Tack the collar in place round the neckline, right sides up. Fit it perfectly by matching all the notches and dots, and by clipping the neckline almost down to the stay-stitching (page 14).

    Now tack the facings, right side **down**, on top.

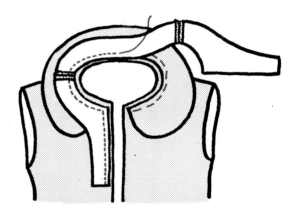

Stitch through all the thicknesses. Layer and clip the seam edges. Turn the facings through to the inside. If there is no facing across the back of the neck, bias binding may be used there instead, from shoulder to shoulder. Turned down and hemmed, it will cover the raw edges of the collar.

2. **Without facings** Tack and stitch the **under-collar only** to the neckline. Layer and clip the seam. Fold in the seam allowance on the **top collar**, clipping if you need to, and hem in place just inside the first stitching.

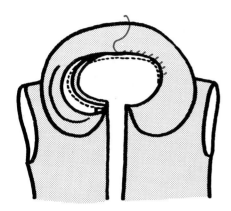

This is the usual way of sewing on **Roll Collars**, especially where there is a neckline zip. The ends of the zipper tape are slipped inside the collar, and the inner edge of the collar hemmed over them. Roll collars must be cut **exactly** on the cross, or they will not set smoothly. (The arrow shows the straight grain.)

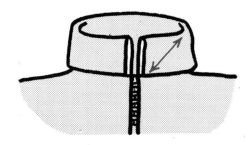

This is also the way to attach a **Tie Collar**. Cut it like a Tie-Belt (page 85). Make the opening, along the lower edge of the tie, long enough to stitch round the neckline—but do not take in any overlap meant for centre-front buttoning.

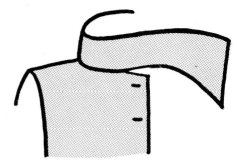

Turn in and hem the loose edge inside the neckline. The collar ends can be cut long enough to tie in a bow, or just to flip over.

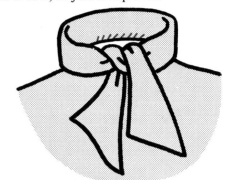

Tailored collars Do not attempt a tailored collar on your first jacket, or until you are sure you can manage it. It needs more skill than the other kinds of collar, and may well be in a thicker, more difficult fabric.

1. **Interface** the under-collar, revers and shoulders, as on page 33. Make all your tailor tacks now.

2. Stitch the **under-collar** to the garment, matching notches and tailor tacks. Press the seam open, and clip so that it will lie flat.

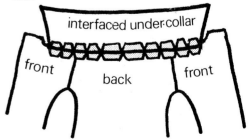

3. Stitch the **top-collar** to the facings, and press the seams open. Clip the facing only at the **outer** end of each seam. Handle carefully, as these parts are not interfaced and can quickly stretch out of shape.

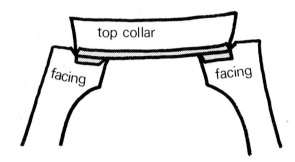

4. Match the facings-and-collar to the garment-and-under-collar, right sides together. Tack carefully, from the lower end of the facing up to the point of the revers. Towards the top of this seam (above the top button of the jacket), the facing edge is usually cut about $\frac{1}{4}''$ (6 mm) **longer** than the jacket edge. Ease this in—it will give the revers more room to roll over.

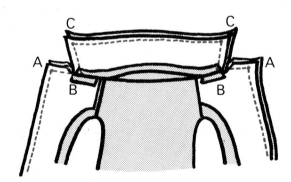

5. Continue tacking as above, round the point of the revers, round the collar, and down the revers at the other end. Be extra careful to match the tailor tacks at the points marked A, B and C, where your stitching will turn corners.

6. Stitch as one long seam, from hemline up to collar and down again. This is perfectly possible if you have pressed and prepared properly—the only way to tackle the difficult parts of dressmaking.

7. Now **layer** the seam edges—the underneath edge in a seam is trimmed more narrowly than the one that will be on top. Layer them to not less than $\frac{1}{8}''$ and $\frac{1}{4}''$ (3 and 6 mm) from the seam. **Trim** across the corners at A and C, and **clip** right into the corners at B.

8. Clip the neck turning of the top-collar at the **shoulder seams**, so that it will fold downwards across the back of the neck.

9. Turn the collar through to the right side. Carefully poke out the corners. To keep the seam out of sight, tack $\frac{1}{4}''$ (6 mm) from the edge of the collar, rolling the seam between fingers and thumb, just to the *under-collar* side. Begin the tacking at the "break-line", where the revers end, level with the top button. Tack up round the collar and down to the break-line on the other side. The top-collar is cut about $\frac{1}{4}''$ (6 mm) wider than the under-collar, to help it roll over better. This also makes it easier to set the collar-seam out of sight. Now tack the fronts below the break-line of the revers; but this time roll the seam just to the *facings* side—the inside.

10. Shape the collar into a smooth curve, by pressing it over a tailor's pad or firmly-folded towel. Use a pressing cloth and take great care not to leave shiny marks. The finished collar and revers should now roll over easily—and *stay* in place.

11. Now tack the loose neck edge of the collar (from shoulder to shoulder across the back), to the turning of the under-collar seam. Tack **only** the edges that have **not** been pressed up into the collar. This will hold the collar and under-collar firmly together along the neckline.

12. When you put in the lining (page 39), it will cover the seam edges round the neckline.

POCKETS

Pockets have to be carefully placed, and the right size to suit your figure and your height. Cut out shapes of pockets or flaps in stiff paper, and pin them to the tacked-up garment at the first fitting. See where they look best, check that their shape suits you and that their size is right.

Remember that pockets draw attention—big hips are not helped by big patch pockets on them: instead, breast pockets might look better. Hip pockets can balance a large bust, and make it seem smaller. Small, neat pockets suit small, neat figures. The taller you are, the larger the pocket you can wear.

When you are sure of the size and placing of your pockets, mark the position of the left-hand one, with a pin at each top corner. Fold the garment down the centre, and mark through both thicknesses with tailor's tacks, so that the right-hand side is marked exactly level with the left. Then there will be no danger of lop-sided placing.

Patch pockets   These are the easiest of all. They are best lined with thin material, cut to the same pattern as the pocket. Stitch with right sides together, leaving about 2″ (5 cm) open along one side.

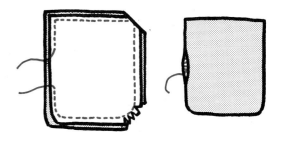

Trim the seam edges, clip the corners, turn through the opening to the right side, and press.

Slip-stitch together the sides of the opening, and top-stitch the pocket in place.

Patch pockets are useful for skirts or trousers; or for breast or hip pockets on shirts.

Patch pockets the professional way This method, used on the best ready-to-wear clothes, gives a much finer finish. The pocket is stitched on, all the way round, from its **inside**. This is difficult because you cannot tack the pocket into place before machining—so do not try it unless you can machine with the help of just one pin at a time.

1. First cut a **pocket pattern**, the size of the finished pocket, from cardboard or thick Vilene. It should not be smaller than about 6″ (15 cm) across, and should have rounded corners. Cut five deep, **evenly-spaced** notches round each lower corner, just wide enough to mark through with tailor's chalk.

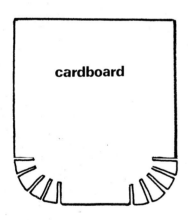

2. Put this pattern in place on the garment, and mark all round it with tailor's chalk. Chalk also along each notch.

3. Now cut the **pocket lining** from the cardboard pattern, and chalk in the notches. **Trim off** ¼″ (6 mm) all round the lining to make it *just* smaller than the pocket. **Fold under** ½″ (1·2 cm) along its top edge.

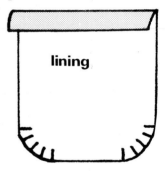

4. Put the lining in place on the garment, matching all the notches. The lining must be **right side down**. Machine in place very close to the raw edges.

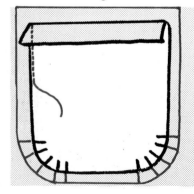

5. Now take a piece of fabric for the pocket itself. Put the cardboard pattern on the **wrong** side of it, and chalk all round. Also chalk in the notches. Cut out the pocket $1\frac{1}{2}''$ (4 cm) **higher** than the pattern along the top, and exactly $\frac{1}{2}''$ (1·2 cm) **wider** than the pattern on the other three sides.

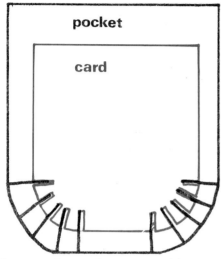

6. Now put the pocket, **wrong** side up, on the garment—to the **left** of its proper place. Match its **right-hand** chalk-line to the **left-hand** chalk-line on the garment. Machine-stitch from the top of the garment marking—A—down to the first notch—B. (The top of the pocket itself will *not* be stitched.)

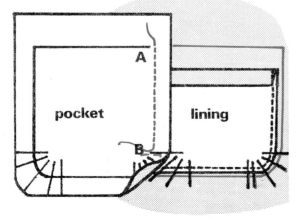

7. With the machine needle **down**, and the presser foot **up**, pull the pocket round so that you match the second pair of chalked notches—put a pin through them, and machine up to the pin. Continue from notch to notch like this, pulling the pocket round as you go.

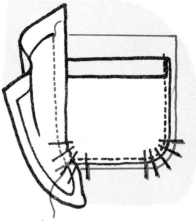

Then machine straight across the bottom of the pocket—round the five pairs of notches at the other corner, pulling the pocket into place at each one—and then machine up the right-hand side of the pocket.

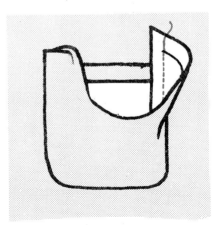

8. Fold in the $1\frac{1}{2}''$ (4 cm) that was left loose at the top of the pocket, then slip-stitch the lining to it on the inside of the pocket.

9. Last of all, **top-stitch** all round the three sides of the pocket, $\frac{3}{8}''-\frac{1}{2}''$ (1–1·2 cm) from the outer edge. This stitching will also catch in the raw edges of the lining, so that you will not be able to feel them rough inside the pocket.

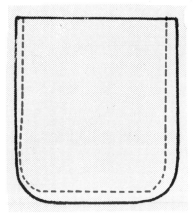

If you can successfully set on a pocket in this way, then you can reckon yourself to be a good dressmaker!

Patch pockets stitched into side seams are suitable for trousers or skirts. Make up the pocket, with a lining, but stitch only the edges that will **not** be sewn into the garment seams.

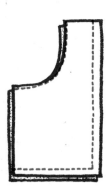

Trim, turn and press the pocket. Edge-stitch the loose edge; then top-stitch the pocket in place, matching the raw edges at the top and side to the edges of the garment piece. They will then be caught into the waist and side seams.

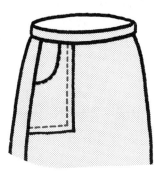

Seamline pockets   Stitch one pocket half to the side edge of the skirt **front**, and the other half to the skirt **back**, right sides together.

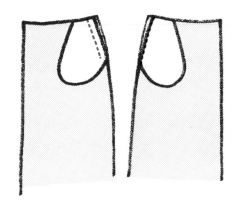

Press both pocket pieces outwards, towards the side.

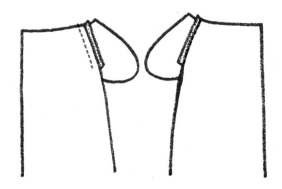

Now tack the skirt pieces with right sides together, and stitch the side seam up from the hem to the lower end of the pocket stitching; swing the garment round on the machine needle, and stitch the pocket seam round and up to the waistline. (Clip the skirt seam turnings where they join the pocket, so that the seam can lie flat.)

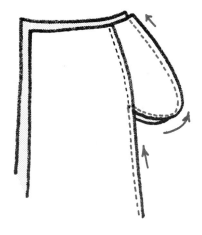

Press the pocket towards the front—the top will then be held together by seaming it into the waist finish.

You may like to cut the skirt seam turnings a little wider at pocket level, so that the pocket seam will be hidden. This is also a useful pocket for trousers.

Zipped pockets in side seams   These are the best pockets of all for school or sports wear,

yet instructions for making them are rarely found. They are not difficult to follow, if you work step by step with the diagrams.

1.   Stitch the **right-hand** side seam of the skirt or trousers, up to the **lower end** of the pocket opening. Press the turnings open along the seamline, right up to the **top** of the opening.

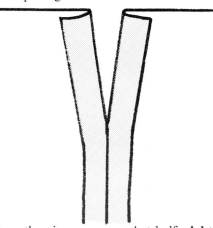

2.   Lay the zip on one pocket half, **right sides up**, and **left edges level**. Machine together along the **left** side of the zipper tape, $\frac{1}{4}''$ (6 mm) away from the teeth.

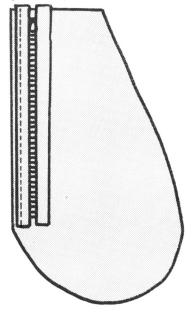

3. Press the pocket half out of the way to the left.

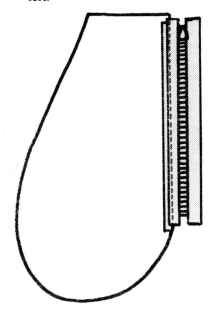

4. Repeat with the other half of the pocket. The zip will now be right side up between the two pocket halves.

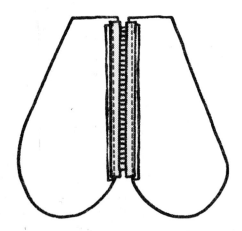

5. Now place the skirt or trouser opening over the zip-and-pocket, right sides up. Tack along the folded edges of the opening, joining them to the zipper tapes, and being careful to keep the pocket halves well out

of the way. Stitch $\frac{1}{8}''$ (3 mm) from the zipper teeth.

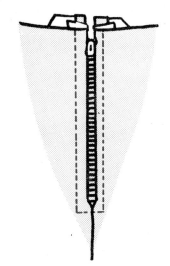

6. Turn to the wrong side.

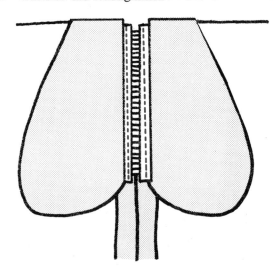

7. Press the right-hand pocket half (as you look at it in this diagram) over the left-hand one. Tack and stitch them together from the bottom of the zip round to the top of the pocket—taking care not to catch in any of the garment. The underneath layer of the pocket will be wider than the top one —trim off the extra, which will be about

$\frac{3}{4}''$ (2 cm). Neaten the edges by zig-zag stitching them together.

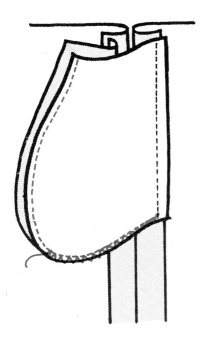

8. Now attach the waistband right across the top of the pocket opening, catching in the top of the pocket pieces and the ends of the zipper tapes. Make a separate opening, in the left-hand seam, with another zip, to get in and out of the garment.

Slot pockets are made in the same way as bound buttonholes.

1. Mark the placing of the pocket on the garment.

2. Cut a piece of fabric for the pocket;
   as wide as the pocket slot will be, plus 2″ (5 cm),
   as long as twice the depth you want the pocket to be, plus 3″ (7·5 cm).

3. Mark the line of the slot across the wrong side of the pocket, $\frac{1}{2}''$ (1·2 cm) **below** the centre.

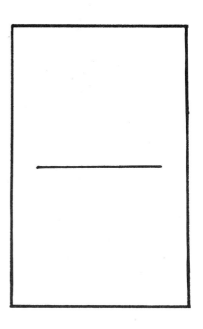

4. Match this mark, **right sides together**, to the pocket marking on the garment. Stitch $\frac{1}{4}''$ (6 mm) above the line—across one short end—$\frac{1}{4}''$ (6 mm) below the line—across the other short end—and overlap a few stitches at the end of the machining for strength. Cut through both thicknesses to within $\frac{1}{2}''$ (1·2 cm) of each end of the slot; then snip carefully right into each corner.

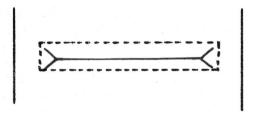

5. Now push the whole pocket through to the wrong side.

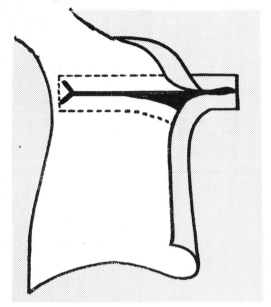

6. Fold the pocket halves to meet, on the wrong side, along the centre of the slot. Pull the two **sides** apart, and they will form little pleats at each end. Catch these down with a few stitches.

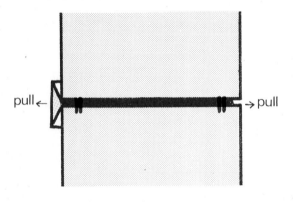

7. Turn to the right side. With the pocket still spread open behind, top-stitch round all four seams of the slot.

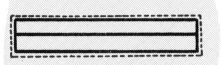

8. Now turn to the wrong side again. Press the upper half of the pocket downwards to meet the lower half. Tack the two layers together along their free edges, and make sure that they lie flat. Stitch them, taking care not to catch in any other part of the garment. For safety, fold it away to the side.

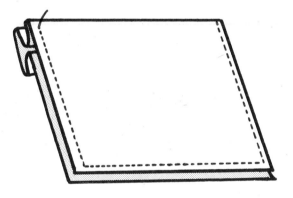

9. If the garment is to be lined, there is no need to neaten the pocket edges; but strengthen the bottom and corners with a second row of machine stitching.

Pockets with welts   A welt strengthens the opening of a slot pocket, as well as making a smart finish to a garment.

1. Tack and stitch the two sides of the welt together, with interfacing (page 33).

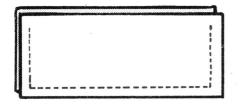

2. Trim, turn and press. Tack the welt **below** the pocket marking, with its raw edges on the slot line.

3. Stitch the pocket piece over the slot marking, catching in the edge of the welt. Turn through and finish the pocket as above, leaving the welt on the outside. Top-stitch the slot round three sides only, as shown. Stitch the fourth side **right on** the welt seam.

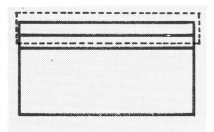

4. Last of all, turn the welt up to hide the slot, and slip-stitch its two ends to the garment.

Pocket flaps can cover a real pocket, or can just give the look of a pocket, without any opening underneath. This may be useful on thick fabrics, where a real pocket might be too bulky—or on loosely woven materials where a pocket might pull out of shape. Or even because you may not be very good at pockets yet.

1. Make up the flap like a welt, and top-stitch, if liked, round the three seamed edges. Then tack the flap, upside down, above its proper place.

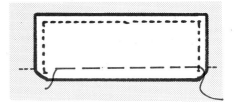

2. Stitch along the unfinished edge, and trim. Press the flap downwards.

3. To make it lie flat, slip-stitch its underneath layer to the garment, $\frac{1}{4}''$ (6 mm) below the machining.

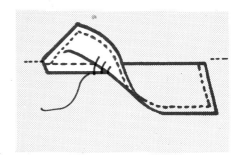

SKIRT OR TROUSER ZIPS

Instead of fitting your zip in the usual way, try putting a fabric shield behind it, to give a smoother fit and to stop it catching on underwear.

1. First cut a strip of your fabric for the shield. Make it as long as the zipper tapes, and 2″ (5 cm) wide. Neaten its side and bottom edges.

2. Lay the zip at the right-hand side of the strip, right sides up, and tack close to the edge.

3. Now stitch the skirt or trouser seam up to where the bottom of the zip will be. Press open the edges of the seam and opening.

4. Lay the closed zip and its fabric shield inside the folded edge of the opening (left-hand as you wear it; right-hand as you look at it here). Bring the fold right up to the zipper teeth, and tack and **top-stitch** $\frac{1}{8}″$ (3 mm) from the fold, starting right at the top of the tape and stitching down to just below the end-stop of the zip.

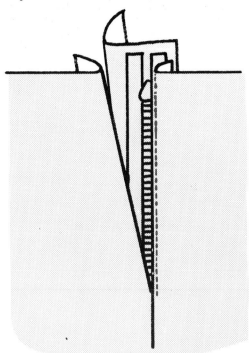

5. Next, pin the overlap edge of the opening to meet the other edge and hide the zip.

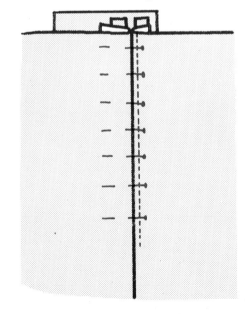

6. Baste the overlap to the free side of the zip **only**, not catching in the fabric shield, which you should push to the side, out of the way.

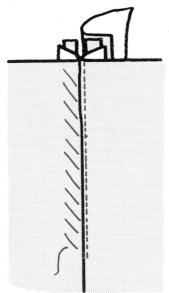

7. Turn over to the inside, and stitch down the right-hand side of the zip, clear of the teeth,

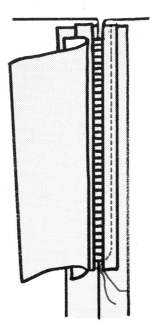

stitching in a curve across the bottom of the tape. Stop at the seamline, pull through the loose ends of thread from the right side and finish them off.

On the outside, the finished zip will look like this:

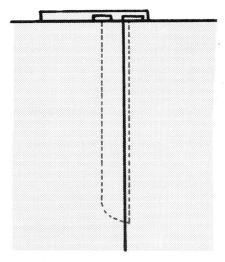

8. Last of all, sew the top of the zipper tapes into the waist finish. It is as well to cut a **wider** seam allowance on the overlap edge of the opening, so that it will be caught safely into the stitching.

HEMS

Blind-hemming by swing-needle machine A great time-saver in dressmaking, so it is well worth your while to **spend** time learning the knack. The hem does not show at all on the right side, if it is well done, and it can be worked on any kind of fabric.

1.   Tack up the hem in a single fold.

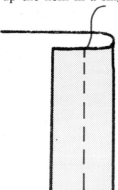

Then turn the hem back on itself, so that the cut edge lies $\frac{1}{4}''$ (6 mm) to the **right** of this second fold.

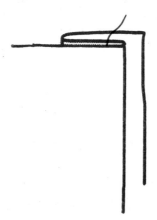

2.   The blind-hemming pattern is built into all automatic and semi-automatic machines. It has one stitch swinging over to the left side, after every five straight stitches.

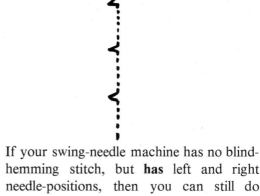

3.   If your swing-needle machine has no blind-hemming stitch, but **has** left and right needle-positions, then you can still do blind-hemming. Simply work five straight stitches with the needle in the **right-hand** position—then, for the next stitch, swing the needle to the **left-hand** position. Work one stitch only, then move the needle back again to the right-hand side. The needle can only be moved right or left when it is **up**, out of the fabric—so this stitch needs to be worked slowly and with care. But it is still a good, neat finish, and quicker than hemming by hand.

4.   Work along the turned-back edge with only the swing-over stitch catching into the garment.

The right side should look like this:

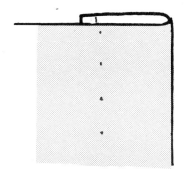

5. An edge-guide for blind-stitching can be fitted to the presser-foot of the machine. This helps to keep the fold in just the right position as it passes through the machine. The knack is to get the swing-over stitch to bite **just** into the fold of the garment. If the stitch is too far to the left, a very long thread will show on the right side. If it is **not far enough** to the left, it will not catch into the fold at all.

Catch-stitched hem   This is the hem used by good dressmakers on thick or woolly fabrics. It makes no ridge on the right side, because it is not stitched over the edge of the hem turning. It is also useful for jersey fabrics, because it is stretchy.

1. First, run a line of straight machining $\frac{1}{4}''$ (6 mm) from the edge of the material—or a line of zig-zag stitching over the edge itself, if the fabric frays.

2. Tack up the hem in a single fold, then turn back the very edge and catch-stitch, working from left to right, and picking up only one or two threads from the garment in each stitch.

   Catch-stitching is done like herring-boning, except that it is worked **between** the hem and the garment, not over the edge. Let

the stitches lie quite loosely between the two layers.

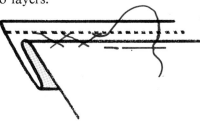

False hem   This is a useful way to lengthen a skirt as a child grows, or when fashion changes.

Let down the hem and press out the creases. Then cut a strip of the same fabric (or lining material), about 3″ (7·5 cm) wide, and long enough to fit round the bottom of the skirt. For a flared skirt, cut a crossway strip. Put this false hem edge-to-edge with the garment, right sides together, and machine.

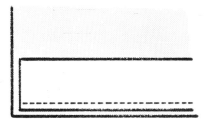

Trim the seam, press it open; then turn up and press the hem to the wrong side. Finish by slip-hemming.

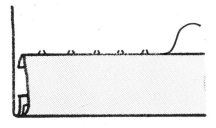

False hems can also be made to turn to the **right** side, when the hem edge would be top-stitched—often a contrasting colour or fabric is used like this.

Rolled hem On very thin fabrics and sheers, a fine edging can be made by rolling a narrow hem. Machine-stitch $\frac{1}{4}''$ (6 mm) from the edge—(on very stretchy chiffon, use a narrow zig-zag)—then trim almost down to the stitching. Roll the edge over between your finger and thumb, and whip over the roll.

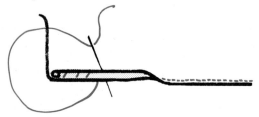

Or slip-hem. The line of machining holds the edge firmly, and makes the hem easier to roll and quicker to work.

Shell-edging is another hand finish for soft or thin materials, making a pretty edge on night-wear. Use a silky embroidery thread, or button-hole twist; and pull up loop-stitches tightly, in pairs, to make the shell shapes.

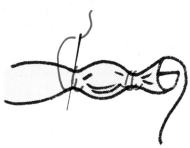

Run your thread inside the fold, between one shell and the next.

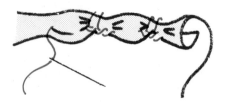

The right side looks like this, with the shells about $\frac{1}{2}''$ (1·2 cm) apart.

Machine shell-edging is a quick finish for thin, soft fabrics such as nylon tricot.

Use the special presser foot for hemming; this will turn the hem over and stitch it at the same time. Set the longest and widest zig-zag stitch you can. Tighten the top thread a little.

Try this stitch first on a scrap of your fabric, as it does not work well on materials that are at all stiff.

BELTS AND TABS

Tie-belts   Allow plenty of length for the belt to flip over or tie in a bow. Tie a tape-measure round your waist in a bow to see how long your belt will need to be.

Cut this length, and double the width you want, plus seam turnings. Interface, if you like, with the fabric itself or with terylene lawn. Fold the belt with right sides together; stitch, leaving a gap in the middle for turning.

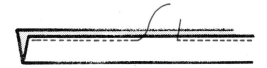

Press the seam to the centre along one side of the belt, then stitch the ends across in whatever shape you choose.

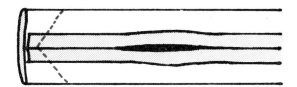

Trim the ends. Turn right side out and press. Slip-stitch the opening.

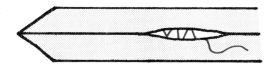

A tie-belt may also be made from a rouleau—see page 90.

Stiffened belts   Buckled belts should be stiffened with belting. (Petersham ribbon is not as good because it creases too easily along the centre.)

1.   Cut the belting the length of your waist, plus turnings of 1″ (2·5 cm) at the buckle end, and 6″ (15 cm) for the slot-through end. Trim the point to the shape you want.

2.   Now cut the covering material about three times the width of the belting, and a little longer. Lay the belting on it and tack them together along the centres.

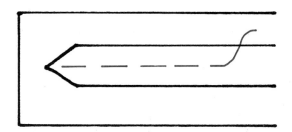

3.   Fold in the long edges and bring the folds to meet at the centre of the belting. Crease the material over the point of the belt and trim off the unwanted edge, allowing $\frac{3}{8}$″ (1 cm) for turnings.

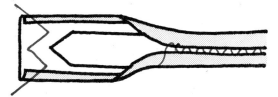

4.   Slip-stitch together the turnings at the end, and along the centre of the belt.

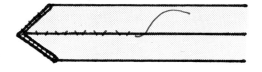

5.   Lastly, top-stitch by machine to make a firm finish, and attach the buckle.

Eyelet holes in belts are put in with a punch. Instructions come in the pack—but be careful to put a piece of wood, or a thick magazine, under the belt while you are hammering out the holes; or you will give yourself a fine set of hole-marks on your table.

Machine-made eyelets can be worked on most swing-needle machines, using a special cover-plate over the machine teeth.

Make up your belt, and cut the hole with a punch or sharp point. Press the hole over the stud on the cover-plate, and set the stitch as the machine instruction book tells you. DO practise first on a scrap of belting with the covering fabric folded over it, to make sure that your machine will make evenly-stitched eyelets.

Half-belts are sometimes fitted across the back of a coat. They should be interfaced, turned and pressed. Top-stitching makes a good finish.

Tack them to the garment back, with edges level and right sides up. Their ends are then stitched into the side seams.

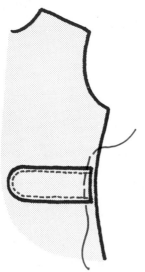

Make the half-belts long enough to overlap—and finish with one or two buttons, sewn through both the halves.

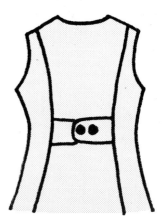

Shoulder and cuff tabs are made in just the same way, with their ends stitched into the armhole or sleeve seam.

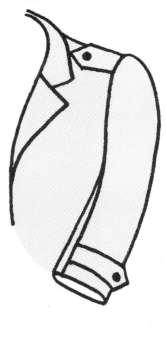

BUTTONS AND BUTTONHOLES

Covered buttons   Cover bought button-shapes with your fabric—or with a contrasting one. Check-covered buttons on plain fabric, or the other way round, can be eye-catching. Follow the instructions on the pack—but with thin fabrics it is best to use a piece of soft material also, as a lining. Tack both thicknesses together first, and use as one. This stops the metal shape from showing through.

Button-snaps are buttons built on top of press studs. They are good for fastening jacket fronts, if there is not much strain on them; and they save making buttonholes on leather or heavy denim. Do not use them where a sudden movement might make them pop open—they are not firm enough for waistbands.

Buttonholes   Perfectly-made **machine button- holes** look well on any garment. They are so useful that you *must* master the knack of doing them.

Some automatic buttonholes, made without having to turn the garment during stitching, may come out unevenly stitched along the two sides—unless the machine is perfectly adjusted. If you have been disappointed with your buttonholes, first check with your machine instruction book that you are following its directions **exactly**.

If you still have trouble, try this old-fashioned but sure-fire method of making perfect button-holes every time. It is not difficult if you follow these instructions carefully; and it can be worked with any make or model of swing-needle machine, so long as it has a **left-hand** position for the needle.

First, make a trial buttonhole, to get the feel of it, on a scrap of your fabric, doubled and interfaced in the same way as the garment.

1. Use the special buttonhole foot, with a rib down the middle to keep the two sides of the buttonhole apart. Loosen the top thread a little.

2. Set the stitch width at **slightly less than half** the widest possible one.

3. Set the stitch length short enough to make a good satin-stitch.

4. Move the needle into the **left-hand** position.

5. Work down the **left** side of the buttonhole, ending with the needle **down** in the fabric, at the **right-hand side**; shown here by the dot.

6. Lift the presser foot, swing the work round on the needle, and lower the presser foot again. You are still at the dot.

7. Now **lift the needle** out of the work. Change the stitch to the **widest** possible width. (If the needle is down when you move it, it will pull the work out of place, and spoil your buttonhole.)

8. Now hold the buttonhole **firmly** so that it does **not** run through the machine, and work 6–8 wide stitches across the end. Finish with the needle **up**.

buttonholes than the less shiny threads. **Buttonhole twist** is very good on thick fabrics, but needs practice to get the best results.

9. Set the **narrower** stitch width again.

10. Machine down the second side, making sure that you **begin to move** straight away. This is the point where a knob of thread can easily build up, if you have done too many stitches across the end; and it may stop your stitching from moving along.

11. Take care to leave a thread or two of fabric showing between the two sides of the buttonhole, where it will be slit open.

12. At the end of the buttonhole, **raise the needle** out of the work, and set the **widest** stitch again.

13. Repeat No. 8 above, to finish the button-hole.

14. Now pull the ends of thread through to the wrong side, tie them, and thread them away between the thicknesses of fabric.

15. Cut your buttonhole open with a seam-ripper, working always from the **ends** to **middle** in case of accidents.

16. **Machine embroidery thread** makes better

CASINGS

Casings are needed to hold in place the elastic, or ribbon, which is threaded through them.

Casings in hems can be used on pyjama trousers, blouse wrists, etc. Turn the hem, and machine close to **both** folds to make it lie flat. Leave a gap of 1″ (2·5 cm) in the lower line of stitching, to thread in the elastic;

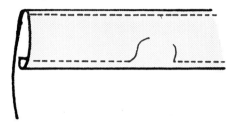

or make a buttonhole on the inside layer, before turning the hem.

Elastic is most easily threaded with a safety pin. Stitch the ends together with a plain or 3-step zig-zag for stretch.

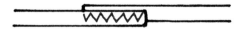

Casings made with bias or seam binding are used where there is to be a frill below the elastic, for instance on a sleeve. Stitch the binding along both its edges on the **wrong** side of the sleeve, **before** stitching the sleeve seam. Thread in the elastic, hold the ends with pins,

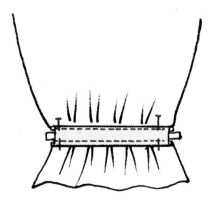

and then catch them safely into the sleeve seam.

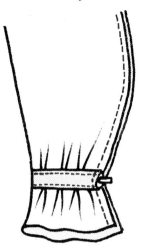

Draw-strings can be used instead of elastic. Make them of ribbon, cord or rouleau—see next page.

ROULEAU LOOPS

(pronounced Roo-Lo) are such a useful fastening that it is well worth the trouble of learning to make them well. As they are made from bias strips, they can be stretched or eased into whatever shape you need, for button-loops, belts, belt-carriers etc.

Cut a bias strip 1″–1½″ (3 cm) wide, and as long as the finished rouleau is to be. Join strips now, if you need to, along the straight grain; as you would join any crossway strips. It is not possible to join them once they are made up.

Fold the bias, with the right side inside, along its length. Machine with a polyester thread and a small stitch, right down the **centre** of the folded strip. Stretch it as much as possible while you stitch. Do not sew close to the raw edges, or you will get a flat rouleau instead of a fat, round one.

If you lay the two ends of the machine threads (pulled out nice and long) **inside** the fold before you begin to sew, you will be able to use them to pull the rouleau through, right way out, when it is stitched.

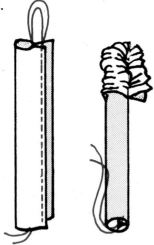

Rouleau strips can be used as **button loops** along an edge with a facing. Make the strip into loop shapes on the **right side** of the gar-

ment, and tack them in place—but facing away from the edge. Snip the sharp folds that will come inside the seam, to make them lie flat. Check that the loops will fit your buttons.

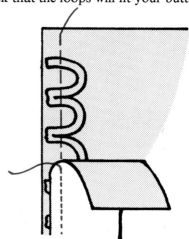

Put the facing on top, right sides together. Machine the seam and turn the facing to the inside, so that the loops come along the edge.

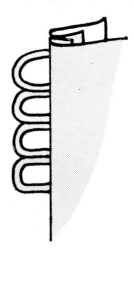

FROGS AND TOGGLES

Well-made frogs can add great style to a jacket—but nothing looks worse than limp, straggly, badly-made ones. The secret is to use a really thick cord or rouleau for the job. It should be fat enough to coil tightly, with only a very small hole in the middle of each loop.

The simplest frogs have three short loops—and a fourth just long enough to slip over the toggle. Coil them as shown, and sew the loops and ends together very firmly on the wrong side.

Stitch a frog to each side of the garment opening, with the middle of the long loop on the centre-line of the garment. Sew a toggle (or button) at the crossing of the loops, on each frog.

LOOPS, TIES AND STAYS

These are different ways of keeping your clothes in their proper shape while you are wearing them, or when you hang them up.

Coat ties are useful for heavy, double-breasted coats, to stop the hem of the left side from drooping and showing the right.

From your lining fabric, make a narrow tie (like a tie-belt, page 85) about a yard (92 cm) long. Fold it in half and stitch the fold to the seam turning of the **right** armhole. Do this when you put in the coat lining.

Now make a 1″ (2·5 cm) thread loop at the left edge of the coat, at bust level.

The ends of the tie can now be slipped through the loop and tied tightly enough to hold up the weight of the left side.

Inside coat buttons   Another way to keep a double-breasted coat in place is to sew an inside button just behind the top right-hand button. Sew them both on at the same time, taking the thread through from the top to the inside button. Work a buttonhole at the same level on the left side, and fasten this before doing up the other buttons.

3.   Then a long one across the bottom;

4.   Repeat, letting the upper stitches become longer and the lower ones shorter;

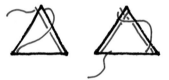

5.   Until the whole triangle is filled up.

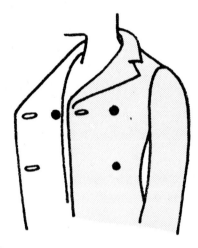

Arrowheads are used to strengthen—and to decorate—the tops of pleats. They are simple to work, and give a beautiful finish to a skirt. You can also use them at the ends of slot pockets.

French tacks are used to hold the loose lining of a coat at the hemline (page 41). They are loop-stitched bar-tacks, worked between the lining and coat hems, at the back and side seams.

1.   Chalk a triangle across the top of a pleat —about the size it is shown here.

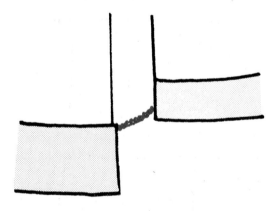

2.   Using a silky buttonhole twist, bring up the needle at the bottom left-hand corner. Take a tiny stitch across the top of the triangle;

Make them $\frac{1}{2}''$ (1·2 cm) long, and they will hold the lining down without pulling.

Waist stays can be put inside fitted dresses with full or heavy skirts, to hold the waistline in place. Make a firmly-fitting belt of petersham ribbon (or wide elastic), hooked together at the ends.

Catch this belt to the seam-turnings inside the waistline, with $\frac{1}{4}''$ (6 mm) French tacks.

Place the hooked ends under the zip and catch them to the edges of the zipper tapes.

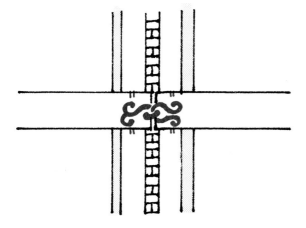

Belt-carriers can be made from straight-grain strips of the garment fabric, about $1\frac{1}{4}''$ (3 cm) wide, folded and machine-stitched.

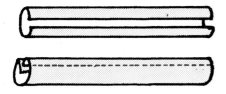

1. Make one long strip, and cut it up into the number of carriers you need. Make them 1″ (2·5 cm) longer than the width of the belt, to allow for the turnings at the ends, and for slack round the belt.

2. At each side seam, machine a carrier upside down above its proper place.

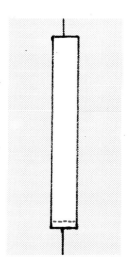

3. Fold it downwards, turn up the lower end, and stitch. This also can be done by machine, if you pin the carrier to one side.

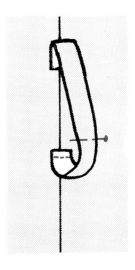

4. When fixing carriers with just a short run of machining, it is firmest to stitch from the

93

middle to one edge—then to the other edge —then back again to the middle.

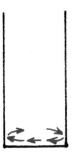

5. Belt-carriers can also be made from rouleau strips, stitched into the side seam; or from thread loops, or chain crochet.

Coat hangers, stitched along the seam at the back neckline, are made like belt-carriers. Use the coat lining fabric, but for strength cut it along the selvedge. Stitch on very firmly, with loop and back-stitching, leaving a little ease for hanging up.

Coat hangers may, instead, be machined into the neckline seam, between the collar and the back facing.

Shoulder strap carriers are made from $\frac{1}{4}''$ (6 mm) ribbon or, like coat hangers, from a narrow strip of fabric. They are fastened with press-studs. Place them along the shoulder seams, with their opening ends towards the neck, so that they are easy to fasten. Stitch them to the seam turnings only. (Never use safety pins in shoulder seams—they can pull your clothes to pieces!)

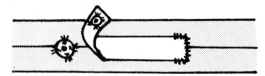

Hanging tapes are loops of tape about 10'' (25 cm) long, stitched inside the waistline of a dress—especially a long, heavy one. Slip them over the ends of the hanger when you hang up the dress. They will take the weight of the skirt, so that it does not pull the bodice out of shape.

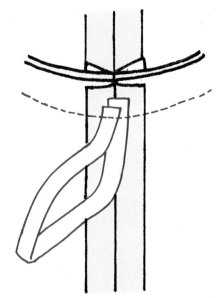

Hanging tapes on *skirts* are stitched into the waist finish, and are just long enough to slip over the ends of a hanger. Make them of the skirt lining fabric.

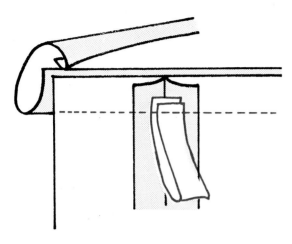

Neckline elastics Very low, wide-cut necklines are sometimes difficult to wear, as they fall forwards and let bra and shoulder straps show. Wedding and party dresses often have this fault.

The cure is simple. Take two pieces of narrow elastic, each about 32″ (82 cm) long, and stitch one end inside each neckline corner. Thread them to each side, **under** your bra straps; round under your arms, crossing behind your back; and right round to the front again, hooking their ends together at your waist. Your neckline will be held perfectly in place, and your straps stay hidden.

7 DRESSMAKING WITHOUT A MACHINE . . .

There are very many people who make good clothes—for themselves as well as for children —without using a machine at all. We do not often realise this, as hand-sewn garments can look just the same on the outside.

Of course a machine is the greatest possible help; but if you cannot have one just now, learn the skill of hand sewing and make beautiful clothes without one. After all, fine clothes have been made by hand all down the ages; but the first domestic sewing machines were made little more than a hundred years ago. Hand stitching is still the mark of the best clothes of all—but you **do** need patience.

SEAMS

Machined seams are strong because they are stitched with two threads, and with many stitches to the inch. So with hand-stitching, always use a polyester thread—on **any** fabric —for stretch and strength. Cotton threads are not really strong enough; and a double thread does not help because it tangles so easily, and delays you.

Work with tiny, even, running stitches, as small as you can get them, so that there are about 5 stitches, and 5 spaces between them, to each inch. (2 to each centimetre.) Take a back-stitch every 6–8 stitches, for extra strength, and mind that you do not pull the whole seam up too tightly. It should lie as flat as a machined seam.

Keeping in a straight line may be difficult at first; this will come quite soon with practice.

Be very careful to start and finish off your seams securely—these are the danger points in hand-made garments.

Seams that take strain—such as round arm-holes—should be all back-stitched, to give them some stretch. So should seams on **jersey fabrics.**

Seams on thick fabrics should be neatened by overcasting.

Seams on thin fabrics and sheers are often better hand-sewn than machined. Use French seams. If you have a use a flat seam, neaten it by pressing a narrow fold along each edge—then work a running stitch along the fold.

FASTENINGS

Zips can be set in more neatly by hand than by machine—in the most expensive clothes, they are usually hand-set. The stitches need not show so much; use back-stitching, with only a tiny stitch on the right side, and the longer stitch hidden underneath.

Bound buttonholes, and other fastenings such as *rouleau loops*, can be worked just as well by hand; backstitched all the way for strength.

TWO USEFUL HAND STITCHES

Blind back-stitch   Place two folded edges together, touching along the folds. Take a stitch forward in one fold, just through the thickness of the fabric along the fold.

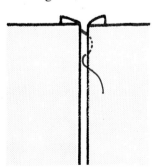

Then take a stitch **half as long** in the other fold, starting right opposite where you came out, but going **backwards**.

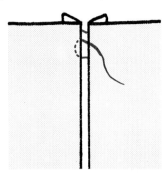

Take a forward stitch in the first fold again, and a small one back in the other.

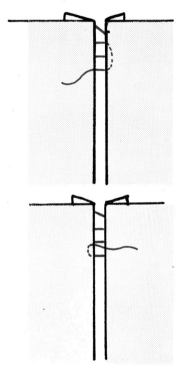

Repeat these stitches, first forwards in one fold, then **half** the distance backwards in the other. They make real back-stitches on the **wrong** side, but are worked from the **right** side. When they are pulled up fairly tightly, they do not show at all, and make a firm seam.

97

Blind back-stitching is useful for mending small splits in seams, where you cannot easily get at the wrong side.

It is also the tailor's way of making some **Inlaid** seams; and of letting in a contrasting fabric on a tailored collar.

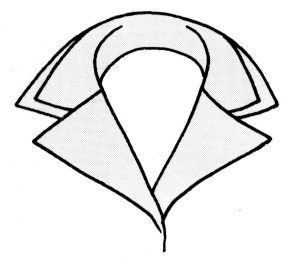

The stitches round the contrasting inlay on the collar, down to the revers, would be impossible to see.

Saddle-stitching   This is used on model clothes instead of machined top-stitching. With button-hole twist (in a different colour if you wish), make bold, even running stitches about $\frac{1}{4}''$ (6 mm) from the edge or seam. These come out a better shape if you make the stitch in two movements—**down**; and then **up** as a separate stitch. Saddle-stitching looks splendid round a collar or patch pocket, or on a yoke or belt.

LEATHER AND SUÈDE GARMENTS

are the only ones that are really difficult to make by hand. (But think—for the price of the leather you could probably buy a second-hand straight-stitching machine. Perhaps one of those marvellous old Singers; see page 103.)

Wash-leather is possible, but only just, with a special "gloving" needle that has a 3-cornered point to cut through the leather more easily. Use buttonhole twist. You will need a thimble to push the needle through to the other side, pull a couple of inches of thread through after it, and then bring the needle back again. You cannot go down-and-up in one movement, so work is slow.

8 ... AND TIPS ON BUYING ONE

WHAT KIND OF MACHINE FOR YOU?

There is no best kind for everyone—it depends on what you want the machine to do for you. Look around before you buy, as a machine is an important piece of equipment that should last you for many years.

To find out which kind will suit you best, ask yourself;

1. **How much do you want to pay**? Do you want the cheapest possible machine; for instance, a good second-hand one? Or do you want the latest and most automatic machine, with price no worry?

2. **How much work are you likely to do, and what kind of work**? A little simple dressmaking? Regular dressmaking, with household making and mending? Fine blouses or children's party dresses, with many fancy embroidery stitches?

3. **Who will use the machine**? Only one careful person? Or will there be children around to have a bash?

Hand machines will do all kinds of dressmaking except buttonholes, neatening, and stretch seams for jersey fabrics; these all need a zig-zag stitch. If you have more time than money, a hand machine may be your answer. The drawback is that only your left hand is free to guide the work. The good point is that you can go as slowly and carefully as you need.

There are very few new hand machines to choose from, and they are little cheaper than the electric straight-stitching models; but a good second-hand machine in a reliable make can be had very cheaply, and might tide you over until you are ready for an electric one.

Electric straight-stitching machines will do everything a hand machine can, much faster, and leave both your hands free. If you already have a hand machine, it can be fitted at small cost with a motor and foot control. Make sure a working light is fitted at the same time; this is a great help and costs little more.

Electric swing-needle machines cost perhaps half as much again as electric straight-stitching machines. The simplest have just the plain zig-zag stitch, that can be made wider or narrower by moving a lever or turning a dial.

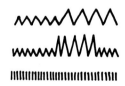

They should also have **centre, left** and **right-hand** needle positions; as buttonholes are much more difficult to make with just a centred needle (page 87).

With these machines, you can;

> Make buttonholes
> Sew on buttons
> Neaten seams with zig-zag stitching
> Make satin-stitched hems or edges
> Make stretch seams on jersey and knits
> Sew on elastic.
> You can also, of course, sew a plain straight stitch.

Some models have the bobbin set in a **free arm** instead of in a **flat bed** working surface; so that you can, for instance, slip a sleeve over the free arm to stitch easily round the cuff.

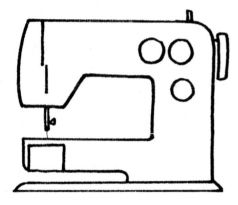

This is a great help for many parts of a garment, and might be more useful to you than extra built-in stitches. (A slot-on extension plate gives you a wider working surface when you want it.)

The advantage of a plain swing-needle machine is that little can go wrong; the more you have built into the machine, the better it has to be adjusted, and servicing can be more of a problem.

Semi-automatic machines are about double the price of electric straight-stitching ones. They usually have at least three stitch patterns built in;

Plain zig-zag,
3-step zig-zag, for sewing stretch fabrics, sewing on elastic, and for mending.

Blind-hemming, very useful because it makes hemming as quick as stitching a seam. (See page 82.)

These models will do every kind of dressmaking; and the three basic stitches also give scope for machine embroidery, especially with twin-needles (two threads on top—one underneath);

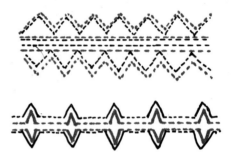

Some semi-automatic models have more stitch-patterns, perhaps including a scallop or an automatic buttonhole. It is a great advantage to have the free arm, as most semi-automatics do.

Fully automatic machines, which cost from three to four times as much as the straight-stitching electric machines, have a very large number of stitches. Some of these have **reverse** stitches included as part of the stitch-pattern, to give extra stretch on jersey seams, or to make fancy embroidery designs. There is also quite a lot more to go wrong: unless you are going to use many of these stitches, balance against them the extra cost, and the extra trouble of servicing.

WHERE TO BUY YOUR MACHINE

Go to a specialist sewing-machine shop. Make sure that they sell a wide range of makes for you to try, and are not just selling one brand. Make sure too that they do their own servicing, and have a good name for it: your machine will need to be checked over once a year to keep it in tip-top form.

Department stores may have machines a little more cheaply sometimes, as "special offers". These are often reliable machines; but they may not work out cheaper in the long run, as department stores are not usually able to service them. Sewing machines do need handling by experts.

If you buy second-hand, try to get a servicing guarantee for three months, and make sure that spare parts are still being made. Your old machine will usually be taken in part exchange, later, for a new one.

POINTS TO WATCH WHEN BUYING

1. The mark of a good machine is **smooth** and **quiet** working.

2. It should be a **recognisable make**, not a nameless machine from an unknown importer; as spares may be difficult to get. (Spares for well-known foreign machines are easy to get, and often fit several makes).

3. **Guarantees** are usually for 5 years for the machine, and 2 for the motor. Avoid guarantees for 10 or 20 years; only the cost of new parts will be included, not the far higher labour charges. Such guarantees are useless, and no honest one could be expected to run for so long. There are firms which rely on these high labour charges to keep them in business. Free after-sales service is the best guarantee of all.

4. **A free lesson** should be given in the shop, so that you really understand how your machine works, **before** you take it home.

5. Check these points while working the machine:

For all machines
    Has the Instruction Book full details?
    Are they clear?
    Is threading easy?
    Can you go as slowly as you want?
    Is the stitch even and straight?
    Can it be made long enough for gathering?
    Is the reverse stitch well made?
    Is the presser foot easily changed?
    Does the machine sew very thick and very thin fabrics equally well?

For swing-needle machines
    Has it a well-placed working light?
    Will it make a smooth, even satin-stitch?

Has it the three needle positions?
Does it make a good buttonhole?

For semi-automatic machines

Does it make at least the three basic dressmaking stitches?

Has it a free arm?

Is there a full set of attachments, accessories and tools, neatly packed with the machine?

SOME WELL–KNOWN AND RELIABLE MAKES OF SEWING MACHINE

The design of sewing machines is changing all the time, so be sure to look for the latest. Meanwhile, here are some tips from practical experience.

Bernina Made in Switzerland, these are excellent machines, beautifully finished, that work smoothly and make an even and reliable stitch. They are simple to thread and have an easily-changed clip-on presser foot.

Working speed can be made so slow that there is no need for a low gear, although some models do have one. They make beautiful buttonholes, better than the "automatic" ones of many other makes. The 5-stitch semi-automatic model also has a scallop stitch, very useful for edging.

Elna Another first-class Swiss make. These machines are equally smooth and reliable. A device to cut down the motor speed can be fitted, especially for beginners, so that both the top speed and the lowest speed are scaled down. Even without this, the lowest speed can be made very slow; but the top speed can be the fastest of any brand of machine—1,500 stitches a minute.

The simplest Elna swing-needle machine can be converted to **semi-automatic** by having some of its parts exchanged later on; then, if wanted, it can be converted again to **automatic**, or to **fully automatic**, each time by paying the difference and having the new working parts fitted. You might find this a valuable arrangement, especially if you are buying your first machine; or before you have decided just how automatic you want to be.

Elna fully automatic machines have the greatest number of embroidery stitches of any make —about 200. The most-used dressmaking stitches are built-in; the others are fitted, as needed, by putting in a cam (the small notched disc that is the key to the pattern).

Elna Lotus is the "Mini" of the sewing machine world. It is the lightest machine, weighing only 14 lbs. Its carrying case is in one with the machine—to open the case, drop down the side and end flaps, which then form a wider working surface. The carrying handle, and the box for tools and accessories, are built tidily into the top of the machine. This grand little model looks like a toy, but it most certainly is not.

The Japanese makes   In the middle-priced range of machines, these Japanese makes are very good value indeed:

Alfa
Crown Point
Frister & Rossmann
Jones
New Home
Toyota

All these brands are reliable and well-made, with easily obtained spares, and very reasonably priced.

Which? magazine chose the Frister & Rossmann plain zig-zag model as its best buy, in 1970, for machines in that class. It is excellent value for money; but as this particular model has one needle position only, button-holing is more difficult than on other Frister & Rossmann models.

Necchi   This is another first-class make, from Italy. One of its models is the heaviest and most strongly built of all the domestic machines, for hard and continuous work—such as out-workers' dressmaking and soft furnishing. A lighter model, the semi-automatic Necchi Lydia, has the special advantage of making some of the back-stitch patterns that are otherwise found only in the more expensive fully-automatic models.

Pfaff   Made in West Germany, they are trouble-free, lightweight machines of excellent quality. This is the first domestic machine with "dual feed", a device used in industry to bring the top layer of fabric through the machine at the same rate as the bottom layer. It helps to give faster and more exact working, particularly on difficult slippery materials, or those with a pile or nap.

Another good point is that there is no loss of power when working very slowly. Their special "jam-proof" working is good.

Singer   Made in Britain. Singers are very good machines, with the advantage of servicing and repairs through their own shops all over the country.

If you want the most reliable and cheapest **second-hand** machine of all, choose a **really old** Singer—black, painted with gold pretties. These splendid hand machines never die—they simply go on working perfectly for 50 years or more. They will sew anything from heavy tent canvas to fine silk; in that way, they are better than many modern machines. Be sure to choose one with a round bobbin. You cannot now get spares for the even older long-bobbin machines, so they are not a good buy—but if there is one in the family already, cherish it; it may still have many years of good service ahead!

Viking Made in Sweden. These are perhaps the easiest to use and most strongly made of all the swing-needle machines. They are ideal for school work and for beginners, because they have an excellent slow gear—most useful for difficult bits, however skilled you are. The mechanism is shock-proof, jam-proof and as near fool-proof as any can be. If you **must** drop your machine on the floor, this is the one most likely to survive the treatment.

Some models have bearings of sintered bronze, a specially-made metal that will **never need oiling.**

SOME LESSER-KNOWN MAKES OF MACHINE—A Note on Switch-selling

Some machines, sold only through newspaper advertisements, are best avoided—especially if they are advertised as being half, or a quarter, the price of similar models in the shops. Many of these advertisements are just fishing for a "home demonstration"—when the salesman can try "switch-selling". This is what happens.

The advertised "bargain" will turn out to be quite unworkable—perhaps because it can be started or stopped only by a switch, so that it goes either at racing top speed, or not at all. The salesman will stress all its **bad** points, even perhaps that its dangerous moving parts have been known to give serious hand injuries to the user. In fact, of course, he never sells this model; when he has put you right against it, he will show you another one.

This will have none of the faults of the first— it will have many good points, and be offered on hire purchase over a long period. It will seem so much better than the other, that you may not notice what you are being asked to do —to pay a high rate of interest for a very long time; and to buy a very ordinary but heavily over-priced machine, at possibly double what you would pay, in a shop, for a reputable make.

This, unfortunately, is quite legal; but you are not likely to be pleased with your bargain.

The same sort of switch-selling is also common with knitting machines—often with a separate contract for buying your work, to help pay for the instalments on the machine. This is only a bait to get the sale contract signed—the rate paid for the work will be impossibly low; faults will be found with it; and you will soon give up trying to get your money back in this way.

Your best motto is BUYER BEWARE.

INDEX